De

MW00424387

This book is dedicated to my husband, Allen and to our children, who kept encouraging me in the writing of **More Than Soup Bean Cookbook.**

Special thanks to Dick Irwin for the cover picture and to Robert Jimison for the illustrations.

Notice: The information contained in this book is true and complete to the best of our knowledge. All recommendations are made without any guarantees on the part of the authors. The authors and publishers disclaim all liability incurred in connection with use of this information.

Analysis for recipes was done by using **Prucal,** a computerized diet analysis program developed in the **Colorado State University Department of Food Science and Human Nutrition.**

First Printing, April 1990
Second Printing, April 1991
Third Printing, October 1992
Fourth Printing, December 1994
20,000 in print

Revised 1995

**Library of Congress
Catalog Card Number 90-91471
ISBN 0-9625869-2-7**

**STARLITE PUBLICATIONS
2100 W. Drake #295
Ft. Collins, CO 80526
(970) 493-7969**

Table of Contents

Mitie Mixes' Calico Soup Mix contains 11 ounces of limas, navy, northern, kidney, small red, pinto beans and blackeyed and green split peas. It makes a hearty soup for 8 to 10 people.

Mitie Mixes' Fiesta Supreme Soup Mix contains 11 ounces of small red, pinto, black, northern, navy beans and blackeyed, green and yellow split peas. This is a great vegetarian soup, or you can add a variety of meats.

Mitie Mixes' Black Beans are 11 ounces of the finest beans. Their distinctive flavor lends itself to a variety of recipes. They are traditionally used in South American and Cajun cooking.

Mitie Mixes is dedicated to bringing you an excellent product to help you in your quest for healthy products to feed your family.

To order **Calico** or **Fiesta Supreme Soup Mixes** or **Black Beans,** please use the convenient order forms located in the back of this book.

Bean Nutrition

Beans are not only delicious, economical and versatile, they are also very nutritious. They contain dietary fiber and water soluble fiber that helps normalize blood sugar and cholesterol levels. A cup of cooked beans provides about half the dietary fiber suggested by the National Cancer Institute. This is equivalent to the fiber in 10 slices of whole wheat bread or in 3 to 4 cups of other cooked vegetables. This fiber is filling and may help you to lose weight by helping you to eat less.

Beans are classified as one of the five least allergenic foods. Dry beans need no preservatives. You are in charge of what you add to them.

A normal serving of beans can supply as much as 40% of the minimum daily requirement for vitamin B1 and B6, plus niacin and folic acid, building healthy digestive and nervous systems, eyes and skin. They also provide iron to make red blood cells, calcium and phosphorus for strong bones and teeth, and potassium to regulate body fluid and for normal functioning of nerves and muscles. One cup of cooked beans provides more potassium than one banana and more calcium and iron per cup than 3 ounces of cooked meat.

Beans, when combined with foods that complement their amino acids, such as rice, cornbread, or crackers, form a complete protein, with a fraction of the calories and none of the fat of beef or pork. Soybeans provide a complete protein.

Beans are a near perfect food, superior to bread, cereals, potatoes and pasta as a source of carbohydrates for diabetics. They have a chemical that helps fight the deposit of fat globules in veins and arteries.

Beans contain no cholesterol and very little sodium. They have only about 224 calories per cup -- less than

3 ounces of cooked meat.

Black beans contain 30% more protein and cook faster than other beans, making them a great reason to try black bean recipes!

Dietary guidelines given by the American Heart Association are as follows:

Reduce total fat intake to 30% or less of total calories.

Reduce cholesterol intake (300 mg/day).

Avoid excessive sodium in the diet (3000-4000 mg/day).

In a nutshell—beans offer this remarkable combination of qualities:

High in complex carbohydrates.

High in protein.

High in dietary fiber.

Low in fat, especially saturated types.

Low in sodium.

No cholesterol.

Our recipes do not call for salt. Please taste before adding any, see if they will satisfy without putting it in.

BEANS...
...HEALTH

Cooking Tips

There are two methods of soaking beans:

1. Wash and sort beans to remove any debris. Put in a large pan with 6 cups of water for each pound of beans. Let stand overnight. 2. To quick soak, bring to a boil, boil for 2 minutes. Allow to soak for 1 hour.

In extremely hard water, stir fry presoaked beans in salad oil 10 minutes, then cook as usual. This will shorten cooking time.

Soaking cuts cooking time by half and saves nutrients that prolonged cooking can destroy. Do not add salt to soaking water. It toughens skins and prevents water absorbtion. Add no more than $\frac{1}{8}$ teaspoon baking soda. More than that will darken beans and give a bad flavor.

There is no need to soak lentils or split peas. Anasazis® and limas cook quicker than most beans, and at lower elevations, rarely need to be soaked.

Anasazi® beans lend themselves to any recipe that calls for beans. Like Black Beans, they have a sweetness not present in other beans.

On top of the stove, cook beans in a large kettle. Cover, bring to a boil, add 2 tablespoons salad oil to prevent foaming. Simmer 3 hours or till tender.

At high altitudes, beans take longer to cook. The following methods work well.

In a crockpot, heat on high till very hot, lower heat and cook beans 6 to 8 hours or overnight.

In a 6-quart pressure cooker, use 4 cups water. You can add other soup ingredients, but keep liquid level below one third full and add 1 tablespoon salad oil to prevent clogging the steam vent. Close cover securely, place pressure regulator on vent pipe and cook 30 minutes with regulator rocking slowly. Let pressure drop of its own accord or follow manufacturer's directions.

When using a pressure indicator, heat to boiling after soaking, let steam escape for 1 minute. Put on pressure indicator and over low heat, bring pressure up to 15 pounds for 28 minutes. Set off heat and let pressure drop gradually. Beans continue to cook as it cools.

Microwaves are great for heating cooked beans, but not for cooking dry beans. Beans need to simmer slowly, with plenty of water to soften.

Beans soften and get tender in an alkaline environment. Acid slows down cooking, so add tomatoes or vinegar when beans are nearly done. The calcium in molasses has the same effect. Do not add salt until beans are tender! Otherwise they will not soften.

Always keep beans covered with liquid when cooking. They will not soften if they dry out.

Leftover beans can be kept in the freezer for at least a year. This allows you to cook a large recipe, then freeze in individual containers for quick meals on busy days.

Uncooked beans should be stored in airtight bags or jars, in a cool, dry place, not in the refrigerator. Old dry beans are still good, although they may need to cook longer.

Canned beans may be substituted in recipes, using the guidelines above to determine the amount. You may want to drain and rinse them to remove the added salt.

Our recipes do not call for salt, but it may be added to your individual taste. We suggest you try them without salt first, you will probably find you enjoy the good taste of the ingredients without adding it.

An easy way to chop onions for soup is to put them in the blender with the tomatoes.

Use low fat cheese to lower calories from fat in the recipes.

Dry Bean Measurements

1 pound dry beans = 2 cups dry beans or 5 to 6 cups cooked beans.

Baking With Beans

Baked goods made by substituting some of the flour with bean puree will be more nutritious and more moist. The puree contains a lot of water, so baking time will be longer. Beans are not as versatile as flour, but are well worth trying. The texture may be different, more tender. Remember that baking time must be extended and liquid should be reduced in your recipes that call for all flour.

Purees are made from beans cooked till soft, with no flavorings added. Drain beans, then puree in a food processor till smooth. You can use home cooked or canned beans. If using canned beans, rinse and drain.

Ideas To Cut Down On Flatulence

Don't cook beans in the soaking water. The complex sugars will be re-absorbed. This process does remove vitamins.

Add ½ teaspoon ginger to cooking water.

Add 1 peeled apple or potato, discard when beans are cooked.

Sprout beans: Wash and sort beans, then drain and put into cooking pot. Allow two days to sprout, rinsing each day, then cook by desired method.

The slower you cook beans, the easier they are to digest. Eating beans frequently reduces the gas problem. Your body conditions itself to better digest them.

Serve applesauce or apple salad with a bean dish.

BLACK BEAN CAKE

6 T. cocoa or carob powder
1/4 lb. margarine
3/4 c. sugar
3 eggs, separated
1 T. vanilla
1 c. black bean puree
1/3 c. walnuts, chopped (optional)

Beat margarine and sugar well. Beat in eggs, one at a time. Add cocoa, vanilla, bean puree and nuts; mix just till blended. In another bowl, beat egg whites until stiff peaks form. Gently stir whites into batter. Pour into greased 8-inch round cake pan. Bake in center of oven at 350° for 1 hour. This will be quite moist. Cool in the pan on wire rack 10 minutes. Use a knife around edge and turn out on rack. This is so rich that is does not need icing. May be served with whipped topping.

Calories 190, protein 4.4 gm, sugars 12.75 gm, fiber 2.4 gm, sat. fat 2.4 gm, poly. fat 4 mg, choles. 50.6 mg, sodium 106.6 mg, potas. 146.4 mg. Analysis for 1/12 of recipe.

Yes! There is no flour in this recipe!

DESSERTS

PINTO BEAN CANDY

$1/2$ c. pinto beans, cooked & mashed
1 lb. confectionery sugar, sifted
$1/4$ tsp. maple extract
$1/2$ c. nuts, chopped
$1/4$ c. butter, melted
1 c. chocolate chips
Paraffin (size of a walnut)
1 c. pinto beans, mashed

Combine all ingredients, mixing well. Roll into balls the size of a walnut. Chill about an hour. Melt chocolate chips with paraffin. Dip balls into this while it is still warm. Chill again to set the chocolate.

BLACK BEAN BROWNIES

6 T. cocoa
1/2 c. margarine
2 c. sugar
4 eggs
1 c. black bean puree
1 T. instant coffee powder
1/2 c. walnuts, chopped (optional)

Beat margarine, sugar, cocoa and coffee. Add eggs, one at a time. Beat in bean puree. Stir in nuts. Pour into 9 x 13-inch greased pan. Bake at 350° for 45 minutes for moist, fudgy brownies. If you like drier brownies, bake 5-10 minutes longer. Cool completely in pan. Cut into 1 1/2 x 2-inch bars.

Calories 212, protein 3.8 gm, sugars 25.18 gm, fiber 1.75 gm, sat. fat 1.95 gm, poly. fat 3.48 mg, choles. 50.6 mg, sodium 84.37 mg, potas. 114.25 mg. Analysis for 1/16 recipe.

Yes! There is no flour in this recipe!

PINTO PIE

1 c. cooked, mashed pintos
1/2 c. sugar
1 c. evaporated milk
2 eggs
1/2 c. coconut
2 tsp. vanilla

Mix all together and pour into a 9-inch pie crust. Bake at 350° for 45 minutes. Top with whipped cream, if desired.

Calories 343, protein 8 mg, sugars 23.3 gm, fiber 6 gm, sat. fat 5.9 gm, poly. fat 2.5 mg, choles. 69.3 mg, sodium 46.6 mg, potas. 262.5 mg. Analysis for 1/6 of recipe.

FLAKY BEAN PIE CRUST

1¹/₂ c. flour
1 tsp. salt
¹/₂ c. pinto bean puree
¹/₂ c. shortening
3 T. water

Mix all ingredients with a fork or in food processor until well blended. Roll out to ¹/₈ inch thick on floured board. Use with your favorite vegetable or fruit filling.

Calories 285, protein 4.5 gm, sugars .83 gm, fiber 2.6 gm, sat. fat 5.9 gm, poly. fat 3.18 mg, choles. 9.3 mg, sodium 0 mg, potas. 93.8 mg. Analysis for ¹/₆ recipe.

DESSERTS

BEAN PIE CRUST

1 c. cooked beans, mashed
1 tsp. baking powder
1 egg
2 T. salad oil
1 c. flour

Combine as for pie crust. Roll out to ⅛-inch thickness on a well floured board. This will make a soft dough.

Options:

1. Cut into squares; fill with meat and/or vegetable filling. Fold over and seal edges with a fork. Bake at 350° for 45 minutes or till brown.

2. Use as a crust for your favorite fruit pie, using a lattice or cut outs top.

3. Roll out to ⅛-inch thickness; prick with a fork and score into 2-inch squares. Bake at 375° for 14 minutes or till lightly browned. Cool, then spread with cream cheese and top with sliced fresh fruit or your favorite jam.

Calories 150, protein 5.5 gm, sugars .66 gm, fiber 4.3 gm, sat. fat .6 gm, poly. fat 1.5 mg, choles. 33.8 mg, sodium 11.6 mg, potas. 159.3 mg. Analysis for ⅙ recipe.

PINTO BEAN FUDGE

1 c. cooked pinto beans, mashed
3/4 c. margarine, melted
3/4 c. cocoa
1 T. vanilla
2 lbs. powdered sugar
1/2 c. nuts, chopped (optional)

Mix first 4 ingredients. Stir in sugar and nuts. Spread in buttered 9 x 13-inch pan. Store in refrigerator.

Calories 131.8, protein 1.26 gm, sugars 17.1 gm, fiber .93 gm, sat. fat .03 gm, poly fat 2.2 mg, choles. 0 mg, sodium 53.5 mg, potas. 67.8 mg. Analysis for 1/30 recipe.

DESSERTS

PINTO PECAN PIE

2 c. hot cooked pintos, pureed & cooled
2 c. sugar
1 c. brown sugar
4 eggs, beaten
1/2 c. margarine
1 c. milk
1 c. pecans, chopped
1 tsp. vanilla

Mix all ingredients and pour into 2 unbaked 9-inch pie shells. Bake at 350° for 1 hour or till knife inserted in center comes out clean.

Calories 558, protein 9.25 gm, sugars 53.3 gm, fiber 4.75 gm, sat. fat 4.96 gm, poly. fat 8.8 mg, choles. 68.4 mg, sodium 129 mg, potas 320.3 mg. Analysis for 1/12 of recipe.

RED BEAN CAKE

6 T. cocoa
2 T. butter
3 c. kidney bean puree
$1/2$ tsp. baking soda
$3/4$ tsp. baking powder
3 eggs
$11/2$ c. sugar
$3/4$ c. salad oil
$1/2$ c. walnuts, chopped

Mix puree, baking soda, baking powder, eggs, cocoa and butter in large bowl; beat well. Add sugar and oil; mix well. Stir in walnuts. Pour batter into 2 greased 8-inch round cake pans, lined with waxed paper. Bake in 350° oven for 35 minutes or till toothpick inserted in center comes out clean. Cool on racks 15 minutes, then turn out of pans and remove waxed paper. Cool completely.

Icing:

$1/2$ c. margarine
8 oz. cream cheese, softened
1 lb. powdered sugar
$1/2$ c. cocoa

Beat margarine and cheese till smooth. Add sugar and cocoa; beat well. Spread on cake and between layers. Chill cake 1 hour or overnight.

(continued)

DESSERTS

Calories 303, protein 5.25 gm, sugars 25.8 gm, fiber 5.5 gm, sat. fat 2.9 gm, poly. fat 8.13 mg, choles. 4.6 mg, sodium 102.9 mg, potas. 248 mg. Analysis for $1/12$ recipe.

The ideal after-dinner speech consists of five words: "I will do the dishes"!

PINTO BEAN CAKE

2 c. cooked pintos, mashed
2 c. apples, diced
1 c. sugar
$1/4$ c. butter
1 egg
1 c. flour
1 tsp. baking soda
1 tsp. cinnamon
$1/2$ tsp. cloves
$1/2$ tsp. allspice
2 tsp. vanilla
1 c. raisins
$1/2$ c. nuts, chopped

Cream sugar and butter. Add egg and mashed beans; mix well. Add dry ingredients; mix well. Add raisins, apples, nuts and vanilla; mix well. Bake in 9 x 13-inch greased pan for 35-45 minutes or till toothpick inserted in center comes out clean. Bake in 375° oven.

Calories 240, protein 9.18 gm, sugars 8.5 gm, fiber 12.6 gm, sat. fat 2.14 gm, poly. fat 1.75 mg, choles. 20.37 mg, sodium 52 mg, potas. 510.9 mg. Analysis for $1/16$ of recipe.

DESSERTS

MOCK PUMPKIN PIE

2 c. pinto beans puree
3 eggs
1 (13-oz.) can evaporated milk
1 c. sugar
1 tsp. cinnamon
1 tsp. ginger
$^1/_4$ tsp. cloves
1 (9-inch) pie crust, unbaked

To puree pintos, put 2 cups beans and $^1/_4$ to $^1/_2$ cup bean liquid into blender. Blend till smooth. Mix ingredients and pour into pie shell. Bake in preheated 425° oven for 15 minutes. Reduce temperature to 350° and bake 45 minutes or till knife inserted in center of pie comes out clean. Cool; serve with whipped cream.

Calories 426, protein 11.6 gm, sugars 37 gm, fiber 8 gm, sat. fat 3.6 gm, poly. fat 2.6 mg, choles. 103.8 mg, sodium 67.5 mg, potas. 407.8 mg. Analysis for $^1/_6$ of recipe.

DESSERTS

PINTO CUPCAKES

1 c. cooked pintos, mashed
2 c. flour
1 1/4 c. sugar
2 1/2 tsp. baking powder
1 tsp. cinnamon
1/2 tsp. nutmeg
1/4 tsp. cloves
1/2 c. shortening
3/4 c. milk
1 tsp. molasses
1 tsp. vanilla
2 eggs
1/4 c. milk

Mix dry ingredients. Add shortening, 3/4 cup milk, molasses and vanilla. Beat 2 minutes. Add eggs, 1/4 cup milk and mashed beans. Beat 2 minutes more. Fill paper cup lined cupcake pans 2/3 full. Bake at 400° for 20 minutes or till they test done with a toothpick. Cool on wire rack. Makes 20-24 cupcakes. Frost or serve warm with butter.

Calories 168, protein 3 gm, sugars 13.3 gm, fiber 1.45 gm, sat. fat 2 gm, poly. fat 1 mg, choles. 23.55 mg, sodium 30 mg, potas. 82.7 mg. Analysis for 1/20 of recipe.

DESSERTS

TUBE CAKE

2 c. cooked pintos, mashed
1 c. sugar
1/4 c. margarine
2 eggs
1 c. flour
1 tsp. baking soda
1 tsp. cinnamon
1/2 tsp. cloves
1/2 tsp. allspice
2 c. apples, peeled & finely chopped
1 c. raisins
1/2 c. nuts, chopped
2 tsp. vanilla

Cream sugar and margarine; add eggs. Beat well. Add bean puree and beat well. Add dry ingredients. Fold in apples, raisins, nuts and vanilla. Pour into greased and floured 10-inch tube pan. Bake at 375° for 45 minutes or till toothpick inserted in cake comes out clean. Cool and remove from pan.

Calories 212, protein 4.5 gm, sugars 22.8 gm, fiber 4.56 gm, sat. fat .968 gm, poly. fat 2.5 mg, choles. 25.3 mg, sodium 94.18 mg, potas. 238. mg. Analysis for 1/16 of recipe.

To prevent foil or other covering from sticking to cake frosting, stick several toothpicks close to the edge of the cake. They will hold the covering up away from the cake.

DESSERTS

PINTO COOKIES

¾ c. cooked pintos, mashed
1 c. brown sugar
½ c. shortening
2 eggs
¾ c. applesauce
1 tsp. baking soda
1 tsp. baking powder
2¼ c. flour
½ tsp. cinnamon
½ tsp. cloves
½ c. nuts, chopped
½ c. raisins

Cream sugar, shortening and eggs. Add pintos and applesauce; beat till fluffy. Add dry ingredients; beat till smooth. Stir in nuts and raisins. Drop by teaspoon onto greased cookie sheet. Bake at 375° for 15-20 minutes or till golden brown. Cool on rack. Yield: About 36 cookies. **Option:** Substitute chocolate chips for raisins.

Calories 106, protein 1.9 gm, sugars 8.19 gm, fiber 1 gm, sat. fat 1.14 gm, poly. fat 1.23 mg, choles. 12.8 mg, sodium 6.1 mg, potas. 75.25 mg. Analysis for 1 cookie.

DESSERTS

FRIENDSHIP CAKE

1 c. greetings
$1/2$ c. of smiles
1 lg. handshake
$2/3$ c. of love
1 T. sympathy
2 c. hospitality

Cream greetings and smiles thoroughly. Add handshakes. Slowly stir in love. Sift sympathy and hospitality and fold in carefully. Bake in a warm heart. Serve often.

PINTO APPLE CAKE

1 c. pinto puree
1/2 c. shortening
1 c. sugar
1 egg
1/2 c. apple butter
1 1/2 c. flour
2 1/2 tsp. baking powder
1 tsp. cinnamon
1/2 tsp. cloves
1/2 tsp. allspice
1 c. apple, peeled & diced

Cream shortening and sugar till light. Add egg; beat well. Stir in bean puree and apple butter. Add dry ingredients; beat well. Stir in diced apple. Pour into a greased and floured 9 x 13-inch cake pan. Bake for 35-40 minutes or till toothpick inserted in center comes out clean. Cool in pan. Frost with powdered sugar icing.

Calories 192, protein 6.6 gm, sugars 18.3 gm, fiber 2.2 gm, sat. fat 2.3 gm, poly. fat 1.25 mg, choles. 16 mg, sodium 47.6 mg, potas. 101.6 mg.

DESSERTS

BEAN CRACKERS

1 c. cooked pintos, pureed
1 tsp. baking powder
1 egg
2 T. salad oil
1 c. flour

Combine as for pie crust. Roll out to ¹/₈-inch thickness on a floured surface. Score into 1¹/₂-inch squares. Bake on a cookie sheet at 425° for 10 minutes or till golden. Cool and break apart at scored lines.

Options: (Before baking use one of the following.)

1. Sprinkle with garlic salt.
2. Sprinkle with cinnamon sugar.

Calories 51, protein 1.65 gm, sugars .2 gm, fiber 1.3 gm, sat. fat .27 gm, poly. fat .86 mg, choles. 10 mg, sodium 18.4 mg, potas. 48 mg. Analysis for ¹/₂₀ of recipe.

DILLY BREAD

1 c. cooked pintos, pureed
2 T. margarine
2 T. onion, minced
1 tsp. salt
2 tsp. dried dill weed
1 pkg. dry yeast
1 c. lukewarm water
2 T. sugar
$3^1/_2$-4 c. flour
1 egg, slightly beaten
2 T. Parmesan cheese
1 T. parsley, chopped

Saute onion in margarine until tender, but not brown. Stir in puree, salt and chill; mix well. Cool to lukewarm. In a large bowl dissolve yeast in lukewarm water. Stir in sugar. Add cooled bean mixture. Stir in flour to make a stiff dough and turn out onto a lightly floured surface and knead till smooth and elastic. Return dough to bowl. Butter top of dough and let rise till doubled in bulk. Punch down dough and shape into a loaf. Put in greased 9 x 5-inch loaf pan. With a sharp knife, make several diagonal slashes 1/4-inch deep in top of loaf. Brush top of loaf with beaten egg. Mix Parmesan and parsley and sprinkle over loaf. Cover and let rise till double, 30-45 minutes. Preheat oven to 375°. Bake loaf till golden brown and sounds hollow when tapped. Remove from pan; cool on rack.

(continued)

DESSERTS

Calories 232, protein 7.2 gm, sugars 3.6 gm, fiber 3.6 gm, sat. fat .75 gm, poly. fat .86 mg, choles. 20.7 mg, sodium 44.6 mg, potas. 143 mg. Analysis for $^1/_{10}$ of recipe.

Man does not live by bread alone, but by every word that proceeds from the mouth of God. (Matt. 4:4)

SPICY RAISIN MUFFINS

1 c. cooked pintos
3/4 c. milk
2 egg whites
1/4 c. salad oil
1/2 c. brown sugar
1 1/2 c. flour
2 tsp. baking powder
1/2 tsp. baking soda
1/2 tsp. cinnamon
1/4 tsp. nutmeg
1/4 tsp. cloves
1/2 c. raisins

Puree beans with milk in blender until smooth. Put in mixer bowl; beat in egg whites, oil and brown sugar. Add dry ingredients, mixing just until all are moistened. Spoon into paper-lined muffin cups. Bake at 400° for 15-18 minutes or until golden. Makes 12 muffins. **Option:** Use honey in place of brown sugar, reduce milk to 1/2 cup.

Calories 184.9, protein 4 gm, sugars 14.4 gm, fiber 2.66 gm, sat. fat .83 gm, poly. fat 2.79 mg, choles. 17.5 mg, sodium 126. 6 mg, potas. 187.4 mg. Analysis for 1 muffin.

DESSERTS

SPICY BEAN CAKE

1/4 c. margarine
2 eggs
2 c. cooked pintos, mashed
1 c. flour
1 tsp. cinnamon
1/4 tsp. nutmeg
1/2 tsp. cloves
1 tsp. baking soda
4 T. cocoa
1 c. sugar
1 1/2 tsp. vanilla
1/4 c. nuts, chopped
3/4 c. raisins
2 c. apples, diced

Cream margarine; add eggs, one at a time. Beat well after each addition. Add dry ingredients; beat well. Fold in apples, raisins, nuts and vanilla. Pour into a greased 9 x 13-inch cake pan. Bake at 375° for 45-50 minutes **Option:** Frost with maple icing.

Calories 190.6, protein 4.3 gm, sugars 19.75 gm, fiber 4.12 gm, sat. fat 1 gm, poly. fat 1.77 mg, choles. 25.3 mg, sodium 43.1 mg, potas. 225 mg. Analysis for 1/16 of recipe.

MAIN DISHES

PINTO PIZZA

2 c. cooked pintos, divided
1/2 lb. hamburger
1 c. onion, chopped & divided
1 (8-oz.) can tomato sauce
2 tsp. chili powder
1 tsp. cumin
1 lb. frozen bread dough, thawed
1/2 c. green pepper, chopped
1/2 lb. Monterey Jack cheese

Mash 1 cup beans; set aside remaining beans. Brown hamburger with 1/2 cup onion; drain fat. Stir in mashed beans, tomato sauce, spices. Simmer 10 minutes. Pat or roll dough to cover 14-inch pizza pan. Spread with bean mixture. Top with onion, green pepper and reserved whole beans. Sprinkle with red pepper flakes. Bake at 400° for 15 minutes or till crust is browned. Cut into wedges. Top each with a dollop of guacamole. **Guacamole:** Mash 1 medium avocado with 1 clove minced garlic and 1 tablespoon lemon juice. Add liquid red pepper sauce to taste. Stir in 1/4 cup chopped tomato. Cover and chill until ready to use.

Calories 397, protein 20.4 gm, sugars 5.8 gm, fiber 8.12 gm, sat. fat 8.57 gm, poly. fat 1.48 mg, choles. 53.8 mg, sodium 513.8 mg, potas. 673 mg. Analysis for 1/8 of recipe.

SOYBEAN HAMBURGER CASSEROLE

2$\frac{1}{2}$ c. cooked soybeans
$\frac{1}{2}$ lb. hamburger
$\frac{1}{2}$ c. onion, chopped
1 c. celery, chopped
$\frac{1}{4}$ c. green pepper, chopped
1 (10-oz.) can tomato sauce
1 c. hot water
1 tsp. beef bouillon
2 c. rice, cooked
$\frac{1}{2}$ c. sharp cheese

Brown hamburger, onion, celery and pepper. Mix all ingredients except cheese. Place in a greased 2$\frac{1}{2}$-quart casserole. Bake at 350° for 45 minutes. Top with cheese. Bake 5 minutes more. Serves 6.

Calories 385, protein 36 gm, carbohydrates 29 gm, sugars 4 gm, fiber 2 gm, sat. fat 5.6 gm, poly. fat 7.4 mg, choles. 37.6 mg, sodium 433.6 mg, potas. 1133.8 mg. Analysis for $\frac{1}{6}$ or recipe.

BAKED LENTILS & CHEESE

1¹/₄ c. lentils, rinsed
2¹/₂ qts. water
1 bay leaf

Simmer 30 minutes or till tender. Drain and remove bay leaf. Put lentils in a greased 9 x 13-inch pan. Mix the following ingredients and put on top of lentils.

2 c. onion, chopped
¹/₂ tsp. garlic powder
1 c. carrots, sliced
¹/₂ c. celery, sliced
¹/₂ c. green pepper, chopped
1 (16-oz.) can tomatoes, drained
¹/₂ tsp. pepper
¹/₄ tsp. marjoram
¹/₂ tsp. sage
¹/₄ tsp. thyme
1 c. American cheese, chopped

Cover and bake at 375° for 1 hour and 15 minutes. Serves 8.

Calories 105.7, protein 6.7 gm, carbohydrates 14 gm, sugar 4.9 gm, fiber 3.7 gm, sat. fat 1.3 gm, poly. fat .17 mg, choles. 6.7 mg, sodium 60 mg, potas. 407.7 mg. Analysis for ¹/₈ recipe.

MAIN DISHES

CALICO CASSEROLE

1 pkg. Mitie Mixes Calico soup mix

One of the following meats:

3 slices bacon, fried & crumbled
1/2 c. ham, diced
1/4 lb. hamburger, browned

1 lg. onion, chopped
1/3 c. brown sugar
1/2 tsp. dry mustard
1/4 c. vinegar
1/4 c. catsup

Wash beans. Cook in 5 cups water for 2 1/2 hours or till tender. Drain, reserving liquid. Saute onion in 2 teaspoons salad oil or bacon grease. Add sugar, mustard, vinegar and catsup. Cook 5 minutes. Put beans in 13 3/4 x 7 1/2-inch baking dish. Pour sauce over beans, adding reserved liquid to barely cover beans. Bake, uncovered, in 350° oven for 1 hour. **Microwave Option:** Cover loosely with plastic wrap and bake on high for 20 minutes.

Calories 307, protein 10 gm, sugar 123.8 gm, fiber 6.5 gm, sat. fat 1 gm, poly. fat .05 mg, cholesterol 17 mg, sodium 131.8 mg, potas. 749.5 mg. Analysis for 1/6 recipe.

SOUTHERN LIMAS & SAUSAGE

1 lb. baby lima beans
1 onion, chopped
1 lg. carrot, chopped
1 tsp. garlic powder
1 lb. smoked sausage
1 tsp. hot sauce
1 bay leaf
1/2 tsp. thyme
1/2 tsp. pepper
4 c. rice, cooked

Put all ingredients, except rice in a large pan with water to cover by 1 inch and bring to a boil. Reduce heat and simmer 2 hours or till beans are tender. Let set for 2 hours to let flavors mingle. Reheat. Serve over rice.

Calories 384.8, protein 26.8 gm, carbohydrates 55.6 gm, sugar 2.5 gm, fiber 20.6 gm, sat. fat 8.3 gm, poly. fat 2.2 mg, choles. 48 mg, sodium 736 mg, potas. 1081 mg. Analysis for 1/6 recipe.

Let Christ stay through the meal; don't dismiss Him with the blessing.

RED BEANS WITH HAM & SAUSAGE

10 c. water
3 lbs. ham hocks
3 c. celery, chopped
3 green peppers, chopped
3 bay leaves
2 tsp. pepper
1 tsp. garlic powder
1 tsp. hot sauce
1$^1/_2$ tsp. oregano
1 lb. smoked sausage
1 lb. sm. red beans, soaked & drained
4 c. rice, cooked

Put all ingredients, except sausage, beans and rice in a large kettle. Cover; bring to a boil. Reduce heat; simmer 30 minutes, till meat is tender. Remove meat. Add the beans and 3 cups water. Simmer 30 minutes. Add sausage; simmer 30 minutes or till beans are tender. Stir often. Add water, if needed to keep mixture soupy. Remove meat from hocks and return to beans. Heat through. Serve over rice.

Optional rice:

(continued)

MAIN DISHES

2 T. butter
2 onions, chopped
1 tsp. garlic powder
1 tsp. pepper
2 c. rice
4¹/₂ c. chicken broth

In a medium pan, saute onion in butter. Add spices ad rice; stir till rice is well coated with butter. Add broth. Bring to a boil. Reduce heat; cover and simmer 20 minutes or till liquid is absorbed and rice is tender.

Calories 961, protein 50.5 gm, sugar 1.7 gm, fiber 7.7 gm, sat. fat 29.5 gm, poly. fat 7.4 mg, choles. 186 mg, sodium 638.8 mg, potas. 810.8 mg. Analysis for ¹/₈ recipe.

If you want your children to keep their feet on the ground, put some responsibility on their shoulders.

PINTO & SAUSAGE BAKE

2 c. pinto beans, cooked
1/2 c. drained bean liquid
1/2 lb. Italian sausage
2 c. onion, chopped
1/2 tsp. garlic powder
1 T. chili powder
1 c. tomatoes, chopped
2 c. tortilla chips, crushed
1 c. Monterey Jack cheese

Brown sausage in large skillet; drain. Add onions and saute till tender. Add spices, tomatoes and bean liquid. Cover and simmer 15 minutes. Put 1/3 of the chips into 9 x 5 x 3-inch loaf pan. Layer 1/2 of bean mixture, 1/3 of chips and 1/2 cup cheese. Repeat layers. Bake in 350° oven for 30 minutes or till heated through. Let stand 5 minutes. Unmold onto serving plate. Cut into slices and serve. This can be doubled; freeze one. Thaw; cover with foil for first 15 minutes or baking time.

Calories 480, protein 20.5 gm, sugar 5 gm, fiber 7 gm, sat. fat 13.3 gm, poly. fat 1.3 mg, choles. 67.8 mg, sodium 543.3 mg, potas. 471.8 mg. Analysis for 1/6 recipe.

CREOLE LENTILS

1 c. onion, chopped
1/2 c. carrot, chopped
1/2 c. celery, chopped
2 T. margarine

Saute the above ingredients 10 minutes in medium pan. Add:

1 (16-oz.) can tomatoes
1 (10-oz.) pkg. frozen cut okra
1/4 tsp. pepper
1 c. lentils, cooked & drained
Few drops hot pepper sauce

Cover and simmer 30 minutes or till veggies are tender. Serve over rice. Makes 5 1/2 cups.

Calories 577, protein 9 gm, sugars 10.2 gm, fiber 8 gm, sat. fat 1.2 gm, poly. fat 1.8 mg, choles. 0 mg, sodium 287.5 mg, potas. 696 mg. Analysis for 1/4 recipe.

MAIN DISHES

LIMA BAKED BEANS

2 c. dry baby limas, cooked
1/4 c. margarine, cut up
1/4 c. brown sugar
1 T. prepared mustard
2 T. molasses
1 c. plain yogurt or sour cream

Mix beans with margarine, sugar and mustard. Fold in yogurt. Put in a greased 2-quart casserole dish. Bake, uncovered, at 350° for 45 minutes.

Calories 376, protein 16.6 gm, sugars 11.7 gm, fiber 12.4 mg, sat. fat 2.7 gm, poly. fat 3.7 mg, choles. 1.8 mg, sodium 157 mg, potas. 1088 mg. Analysis for 1/8 recipe.

REFRIED BLACK BEANS

1^1/$_2$ c. black beans
1 med. onion, chopped
3 tsp. garlic powder
2 T. bacon drippings
1 tsp. ground coriander
Salt to taste
Monterey Jack cheese, shredded
Salsa

Wash beans. Cook in 5 cups water with onion, spices and bacon grease. Cook 1^1/$_2$ hours or till tender; drain. Mash beans with the back of a spoon. Pour enough salad oil to cover bottom of large skillet. Add half of bean mixture; fry. Repeat with remaining beans. Top refried beans with cheese and salsa. Makes 8 servings. This can also be served over taco chips or in any recipe calling for refried beans. This may be frozen.

Calories 289, protein 4 gm, sugars 2 gm, fiber 4.8 gm, sat. fat .87 gm, poly. fat .23 mg, choles. 2.6 mg, sodium 0 mg, potas. 191.2 mg. Analysis for ^{1}/$_8$ recipe.

MAIN DISHES

REFRIED BEANS

1 lb. black or pinto beans, soaked & drained

Add:

6 c. water
2 onions, chopped

Bring to a boil; cover and simmer till beans are tender. Mash beans in blender.

Add (optional):

$\frac{1}{2}$ c. bacon drippings or margarine

Mix well. Cook, stirring often until thickened. To serve in tacos, add 2 tablespoons taco seasoning. To serve as a side dish, add chili powder and cumin to taste. Place in greased casserole; sprinkle with cheese. Heat till hot.

Calories 225, protein 15.2 gm, sugars .75 gm, fiber 22.75, sat. fat .23 gm, poly. fat .4 mg, choles. 0 mg, sodium 133.7 mg, potas. 628 mg. Analysis for $\frac{1}{8}$ recipe. This does not include option.

Maturity means reacquiring the seriousness one had as a child at play.

BAKED BLACK BEANS

1$^1/_2$ c. black beans
6 c. water
1 onion, quartered
$^1/_2$ c. dark molasses
1$^1/_2$ tsp. dry mustard
$^1/_2$ tsp. black pepper
$^1/_4$ lb. salt pork or bacon

Soak beans; drain. Cook beans in 6 cups water with onion till tender; drain, reserving liquid. Place in 2 or 3-quart casserole. Add molasses, dry mustard and pepper. Pour in the reserved liquid so that beans are covered by $^1/_2$ inch. Stir to coat evenly. Preheat oven to 250°. Score the fatty side of the salt pork and push into the beans, leaving the top edge on the surface. Cover casserole and bake about 4 hours, adding more bean liquid if they become dry. **Options:** Use kidney beans, pintos, navies or great northern beans. Add $^1/_4$ cup brown sugar.

Calories 150, protein 18.3 gm, sugars 16.5 gm, fiber 18.8 gm, sat. fat 3.4 gm, poly. fat 1.4 mg, choles. 16 mg, sodium 303 mg, potas. 745.3 mg. Analysis for $^1/_6$ recipe.

Long, slow cooking will enhance the flavor of baked beans.

BLACK BEAN BURRITO PIE

1$^1/_2$ c. black beans
$^1/_2$ lb. hamburger
1 med. onion, chopped
1 tsp. garlic powder
1 (4-oz.) can chopped green chilies
$^1/_3$ c. taco sauce
1 c. Monterey Jack cheese, grated
4 lg. tortillas

Wash black beans; cook in 5 cups water for 1$^1/_2$ hours or till tender. Drain and mash. Brown hamburger and onion in large skillet. Remove from heat. Add garlic powder, beans and taco sauce. In a 9-inch pie pan, place 1 large tortilla. Top with $^1/_4$ of bean mixture and $^1/_2$ cup cheese. Repeat 3 times. Bake for 30 minutes at 350°. Sprinkle with lettuce, tomato and black olives. Serves 6. **Microwave Option:** Use glass pie pan. Heat 10-15 minutes until bubbly.

Calories 528, protein 33.6 gm, sugars .83 gm, fiber 20 gm, sat. fat 11.7 gm, poly. fat 1.2 mg, choles. 70 mg, sodium 206.6 mg, potas. 826.5 mg. Analysis for $^1/_6$ recipe.

BEAN & ZUCCHINI BURRITOS

2 c. pinto beans, cooked & drained
3 c. zucchini, chopped
$1/4$ c. green onions, chopped
1 tsp. garlic powder
1 tsp. chili powder
1 (8-oz.) can tomato sauce
1 (4-oz.) can green chilies
6 (10-inch) tortillas
1 c. cheese, grated

Mash beans. Mix with next 6 ingredients in a saucepan. Cook, stirring often till bubbly. Heat tortillas, then spread $1/2$ cup bean mixture over each; roll up and place in baking dish. Top with cheese. Bake in 350° oven for 20 minutes or heat in microwave for 7 minutes or till bubbly. Serve with lettuce and tomatoes.

Calories 276, protein 15 gm, sugars 5.8 gm, fiber 11 gm, sat. fat 6.2 gm, poly. fat .3 mg, choles. 31.5 mg, sodium 383.3 mg, potas. 759.3 mg. Analysis for $1/6$ recipe.

BLACK BEAN ENCHILADA PIE

1$^1/_2$ c. black beans
1 lg. onion, chopped
1 can cream of chicken soup
1 can cream of mushroom soup
1 (4-oz.) can diced green chilies
1 (8-oz.) can mild enchilada sauce
$^3/_4$ c. milk
1 pkg. soft tortillas
$^1/_2$ lb. cheddar cheese, grated
$^1/_2$ lb. Monterey Jack cheese, grated
1 pt. sour cream

Wash and cook beans 1$^1/_2$ hours, until tender; drain. Mix next 6 ingredients with beans. Place 6 tortillas in greased 9 x 13-inch pan. Top with half the bean mixture and half the cheeses. Repeat the layers. Bake at 350° for 40 minutes. Cool slightly and cut in squares. Top each square with sour cream. Serves 8-10. **Microwave:** Use glass baking dish. Cover with plastic wrap. Cook on high 15 minutes or till bubbly.

Calories 575, protein 30.6 gm, sugars 10 gm, fiber 16.25 gm, sat. fat 13.9 gm, poly. fat 2.6 mg, choles. 69.8 mg, sodium 1144.7 mg, potas. 857 mg. Analysis for $^1/_8$ recipe.

BEANS IN CHEESE SAUCE

1$1/2$ c. black beans or Calico or Fiesta soup mix
1 T. margarine
1 T. flour
1 c. milk
1 tsp. prepared mustard
1 c. American or cheddar cheese, grated
1 tsp. Worcestershire sauce
$1/2$ tsp. pepper

Cook beans and drain. Melt margarine over low heat; stir in flour and milk to make a smooth sauce. Add spices and cheese; stir till cheese melts. Stir in beans. Heat over low heat until bubbly.

Calories 355, protein 22.5 gm, sugars 3.5 gm, fiber 18.6 gm, sat. fat 7.7 gm, poly. fat 1.4 mg, choles. 37.8 mg, sodium 261.3 mg, potas. 615.6 mg. Analysis for $1/6$ recipe.

BLACK BEANS OVER RICE

3 c. cooked black beans
6 slices bacon
1 lg. onion, chopped
1 green pepper, chopped
2 c. rice, cooked

Fry and crumble bacon. Saute onion and green pepper. Add beans with liquid and salt and pepper to taste. Serve over rice.

Calories 223, protein 11.2 gm, sugars 1.2 gm, fiber 12.2 gm, sat. fat 1.2 gm, poly. fat .6 mg, choles. 6 mg, sodium 113.3 mg, potas. 400 mg. Analysis for $1/6$ recipe.

A diet is the penalty we pay for exceeding the feed limit.

CHICKEN & BEAN ENCHILADAS

3 c. plain yogurt
1 c. chicken, diced & cooked
1 (4-oz.) can chopped green chilies
$1/2$ c. onion, chopped
1 tsp. chili powder
$1^{1}/2$ c. sharp cheese, grated
2 c. refried beans
1 (8-oz.) can tomato sauce
1 pkg. tortillas

Spread $1/2$ cup yogurt in 9 x 13-inch baking dish. Mix $1/2$ cup yogurt, chicken, drained green chilies, onion, beans, tomato sauce and seasonings. Spread each tortilla with $1/4$ cup mixture and place seam side down. Top with the remaining yogurt and cheese. Bake at 400° for 20 minutes, until cheese melts. **Microwave Option:** Place in glass baking dish. Cover with plastic wrap. Cook on high for 8 minutes. Makes 6 servings.

Calories 276, protein 26.8 gm, sugars 11.6 gm, fiber 9.3 gm, sat. fat 5.5 gm, poly. fat 1.3 mg, choles. 45.8 mg, sodium 956.6 mg, potas. 969.3 mg. Analysis for $1/6$ recipe.

MAIN DISHES

BRAZILIAN BLACK BEANS

1¹/₂ c. black beans
¹/₄ lb. pork hock, sliced
¹/₄ lb. chuck steak
1 lb. Italian sausage
¹/₄ lb. salt pork
1 clove garlic, minced
¹/₄ c. onion, chopped
¹/₂ c. tomato, chopped
2 tsp. salad oil

Wash beans. Saute garlic, onion and tomato in 2 teaspoons salad oil; add with beans 2 quarts water. Cook 1 hour or more till beans are tender and sauce is thick. Serve over rice. **Rice:** Brown 1 minced clove garlic, ¹/₄ cup chopped onion, 1 chopped tomato in 2 teaspoons salad oil. Add to 2 cups water and 1 cup rice. Simmer 15 minutes. **Hot Sauce:** Place ¹/₂ cup finely chopped onion in a strainer. Pour 2 cups boiling water over onions. Combine onions with 3 tablespoons salad oil, 3 tablespoon wine vinegar and 3 tablespoons cayenne pepper sauce. Serve over top of bean mixture. Serve with sliced oranges on the side. This is considered party fare in Brazil.

Calories 606.8, protein 25.37 gm, sugars 4.3 gm, fiber 13.8 gm, sat. fat 10.5 gm, poly. fat 7.4 mg, choles. 59 mg, sodium 553.6 mg, potas. 820 mg. Analysis for ¹/₈ of recipe.

VEGETARIAN BRAZILIAN BLACK BEANS

3 c. cooked black beans, drained
1 T. lemon juice
1 T. frozen orange juice concentrate
2 tomatoes, chopped
3 T. salad oil
1 med. onion, chopped
2 green peppers, diced
$1/2$ tsp. garlic powder
2 tsp. cumin
1 tsp. oregano
$1/3$ T. rum flavoring
3 c. cooked rice

Heat oil in large pan. Add onion and saute about 3 minutes. Stir in peppers and garlic; saute 3 more minutes. Add beans, lemon and orange juice, tomatoes, cumin and oregano. Cover and simmer 5 minutes; add water or tomato juice to thin mixture, if needed. Mix 1 cup of the bean mixture with the rum and puree. Return to pan and simmer, covered, about 20 minutes. Serve over rice. **Options:** Add chopped onions, green chilies and chopped tomatoes to the rice. Serve with sliced bananas and oranges.

(continued)

MAIN DISHES

Calories 296, protein 10.5 gm, sugars 4.2 gm, fiber 13.5 gm, sat. fat .98 gm, poly. fat 4.35 mg, choles. 0 mg, sodium 12.5 mg, potas. 542.2 mg. Analysis for $\frac{1}{6}$ recipe.

The only way some mothers can get a few quiet moments is to start doing the dishes.

BLACK BEAN TORTILLA BAKE

1^1/$_2$ c. black beans
^{1}/$_2$ lb. hamburger
^{1}/$_2$ c. onion, chopped
1 (16-oz.) can stewed tomatoes
^{1}/$_2$ c. enchilada sauce
1 tsp. chili powder
1 tsp. cumin
^{1}/$_4$ tsp. pepper
6 (6-inch) tortillas
3 oz. cream cheese
1 (4-oz.) can green chilies, drained
^{1}/$_2$ c. Monterey Jack cheese

Wash beans and cook in 2 quarts water in large pot. Bring to a boil; simmer 1^1/$_2$ hours or till tender. Drain. In large skillet, brown hamburger and onion; drain off fat. Stir in beans and next 5 ingredients. Bring to a boil; simmer 5 minutes. Pour half of sauce into a 12 x 7 x 2-inch glass baking dish. Spread tortillas with cream cheese. Top with green chilies. Fold in half and arrange over sauce. Pour remaining sauce down the center. Cover and bake in 350° for 15 minutes. Uncover; sprinkle with cheese. Bake 5 minutes more or till bubbly. **Microwave Option:** Top with cheese; cover with plastic wrap. Bake on high for 8 minutes or till bubbly. Makes 3-6 servings.

(continued)

MAIN DISHES

Calories 494, protein 28.3 gm, sugars 4.2 gm, fiber 21.5 gm, sat. fat 8.1 gm, poly. fat 1.2 mg, choles. 59.3 mg, sodium 328.3 mg, potas. 1006.8 mg. Analysis for $1/6$ recipe.

HOW TO COOK SOYBEANS

2 c. soybeans, washed & soaked
$1/4$ c. salad oil
$1/2$ c. onion, chopped
$1/2$ c. celery, chopped
2 qts. water

Combine all ingredients in a 4-quart pan. Bring to a boil; cover and simmer $2^{1}/_{2}$-3 hours or till beans are tender. Use in recipes; liquid may be used in soup.

MAIN DISHES

SOYBEAN CROQUETTES

2 T. onion, minced
1¹/₂ c. celery, diced
1 c. tomato paste
5 T. flour
2 T. salad oil
3 c. cooked soybeans, mashed
1 c. cornflakes, crushed
1 egg, well beaten
2 T. milk

Mix onion, celery and tomato paste in medium pan. Bring to a boil. Mix flour and oil gradually; add to tomato mixture. Cook to a thick paste. Cool and add soybeans. Shape into croquettes. Mix egg with milk. Roll croquettes in cornflakes, then in egg and milk. Place on a greased baking sheet. Bake at 400° for 20-30 minutes.

Calories 301, protein 20.8 gm, sugars 6.3 gm, fiber 2.5 gm, sat. fat 1.6 gm, poly. fat .26 mg, choles. 34 mg, sodium 161.8 mg, potas. 993.8 mg. Analysis for ¹/₆ of recipe.

BLACK OR RED BEANS & RICE

1$1/2$ c. black beans or sm. red beans
2 lbs. ham, cubed or hamhock
1 bay leaf
1 T. garlic powder
$1/2$ tsp. thyme
$1/4$ c. parsley, chopped
4 T. salad oil
2 onions, chopped
1 sweet green pepper, chopped
1 c. tomatoes, chopped
1 T. white vinegar
1 tsp. hot sauce
4 c. rice, cooked

In a large kettle, put beans, ham, bay leaf, garlic, thyme, parsley and 6 cups water. Bring to a boil, then simmer, covered, 1$1/2$ hours or till beans are tender; drain. Saute onions and pepper in oil in large skillet. Add tomatoes, vinegar and hot sauce. Simmer and stir till thickened, about 10 minutes. Serve over rice. **Optional Garnishes:** 1 chopped onion, 1 sliced lemon, 1 thinly sliced orange, 2 chopped hard-boiled eggs and sliced radishes.

Calories 643, protein 335.9 gm, sugars 2.38 gm, fiber 15.5 gm, sat. fat 9.98 gm, poly. fat .55 mg, choles. 50.6 mg, sodium 311.4 mg, potas. 405.3 mg. Analysis for $1/8$ recipe.

OUR FAVORITE TACOS

1 lb. hamburger, browned & drained
2 c. refried beans
2 T. taco seasoning mix

Mix together and heat through. Cut up enough of the following to feed the number served: lettuce, onion, tomatoes, cheese. Break up corn tortilla chips. Serve bean mixture, veggies and cheese over chips. Top with salsa. This is an easy way to serve tacos to little ones.

Protein 23.3 gm, sugars 3.16 gm, fiber 6.5 gm, sat. fat 6.38 gm, poly. fat .73 mg, choles. 67.5 mg, sodium 415.2 mg, potas. 540.3 mg. Analysis for $\frac{1}{6}$ recipe.

The pessimist complains about the wind, the optimist expects it to change, the realist adjusts the sails.

SOUR CREAM & BLACK BEAN TACOS

1 lb. Monterey Jack cheese, cut in strips
2 (4-oz.) cans green chilies
2 c. black beans, cooked
2 T. salad oil
1 onion, chopped
1/2 tsp. garlic powder
1 (16-oz.) can tomatoes
1 tsp. oregano
2 c. plain yogurt
1/2 c. ripe olives, sliced
12 tortillas

Heat tortillas in microwave till soft. Place cheese, chilies and beans in center of each tortilla. Roll and place in baking dish. Saute onion in oil till tender. Add tomatoes and spices; simmer, uncovered, for 20 minutes or till slightly thickened. Stir in sour cream and olives. Pour over tacos; cover and bake for 30 minutes at 350°. Makes 6 servings. May be baked 8 minutes in microwave.

Calories 659.3, protein 31 gm, sugars 7.8 gm, fiber 10.6 gm, sat. fat 25.5 gm, poly. fat 4 mg, choles. 111 mg, sodium 490 mg, potas. 806.3 mg. Analysis for 1/6 of recipe.

TAMALE BEAN PIE

Filling:

1 T. salad oil
1 onion, chopped
1 tsp. garlic powder

Saute in heavy skillet. Add:

4 tomatoes, chopped
$1/4$ c. green pepper, chopped
1 c. tomato sauce
$1^1/_2$ T. chili powder
$1/4$ c. ripe olives, sliced
1 tsp. hot sauce

Simmer 10 minutes. Add and heat through:

4 c. cooked black or pinto beans

Crust · mix together:

$3/4$ c. cornmeal
1 c. milk

Bring to a boil:

1 c. milk
1 c. water
1 T. salad oil

(continued)

Slowly add the cornmeal mixture, stirring constantly. Simmer till thick; cover and cook on lowest heat for 15 minutes. Stir in 2 beaten eggs. Cover bottom of greased 2-quart casserole with $1/2$ of the crust mixture. Cover with bean filling. Cover with rest of the crust mixture. Sprinkle with 1 cup grated sharp cheese. Bake for 30 minutes at 350°.

Calories 271, protein 13.13 gm, sugars 8.87 gm, fiber 13.75 gm, sat. fat 2.17 gm, poly. fat 2.44 mg, choles. 9.38 mg, sodium 99.38 mg, potas. 704.8 mg. Analysis for $1/8$ recipe.

Everyone should learn to cook, from their mother or from a book.

BLACK BEAN CHILI PIE

3/4 c. black beans
6 c. water
1/2 lb. hamburger, browned & drained
2 tsp. chili powder
1/2 tsp. cumin
1 (4-oz.) can green chilies, drained
3/4 c. black olives, sliced
1/4 c. green onions, chopped
1 1/2 c. tortilla chips, crushed
1/2 c. Monterey Jack cheese, shredded
1/2 c. cheddar cheese, shredded
1 (2 1/2-oz.) jar sliced mushrooms

Cook beans 1 1/2 hours or till tender; drain. Mix with hamburger, chili powder, cumin, chilies, 1/2 cup of the olives and the green onions. Cover bottom of 9-inch glass pie pan with 1 cup tortilla chips. Spread bean mixture over chips; cover with cheeses, 1/4 cup olives, drained mushrooms and 1/2 cup tortilla chips. Cover with foil. Bake in 375° oven for 15 minutes. Uncover, bake 20 minutes more, till heated through. Serve with lettuce and tomatoes. Makes 6 servings. **Microwave Option:** Cover with plastic wrap. Bake on high 12 minutes or till heated through.

Calories 339, sugars .67 gm, fiber 12 gm, sat. fat 6.9 gm, poly. fat .7 mg, choles. 51 gm, sodium 323.3 mg, potas. 572.6 mg. Analysis for 1/6 recipe.

MAIN DISHES

ISLAND RICE WITH BLACK BEANS

1 c. cooked black beans
3 c. rice, uncooked
1 lg. onion, chopped
1 c. celery, chopped
$1/2$ c. green or red pepper, chopped
1 T. salad oil
7 oz. pkg. flaked coconut or 8 oz unsweetened coconut juice
7 c. hot water

Brown onions, pepper and celery in oil. If using coconut, add 1 cup hot water to it and squeeze out cream. Mix all ingredients in greased large casserole, with tight fitting lid. Bake in 350° for 45 minutes, until liquid is absorbed and rice is tender. Add water, if necessary. May be cooked on top of stove over medium heat for same time. Serves 6-8.

Calories 253, protein 5.5 gm, sugars 9.5 gm, fiber 8.6 gm, sat. fat 5.7 gm, poly. fat 1.4 mg, choles. 0 mg, sodium 21.6 mg, potas. 264 mg. Analysis for $1/6$ of recipe.

CHILI & PASTA

2 lbs. ground turkey, browned & drained
1 lg. onion, chopped
1 tsp. garlic powder
2 (15-oz.) can tomatoes, chopped
2 T. chili powder
$1/4$ c. cocoa
1 tsp. oregano
2 c. cooked kidney beans
2 c. vermicelli
Dash of hot sauce
1 c. cheese, grated

Mix first 7 ingredients in a large heavy pan. Bring to a boil. Cover and simmer 1 hour. Add beans, vermicelli and 1 cup water. Return to a boil. Cover and simmer 30 minutes more. Sprinkle each bowl of chili with cheese. Serves 8.

Calories 524, protein 44 gm, sugars 5.6 gm, fiber 7 gm, sat. fat 6 gm, poly. fat 2 mg, choles. 114 mg, sodium 251.2 mg, potas. 871.8 mg. Analysis for $1/8$ recipe.

MAIN DISHES

BEAN LUNCH PANCAKES

2 T. salad oil
3 c. cooked pintos, drained
2 eggs
4 scallions, sliced thin

In blender, puree beans with eggs; pour into bowl. Add scallions. Heat oil in skillet over medium heat. Pour 2 tablespoons batter into hot skillet. Fry 2-3 minutes, then turn; fry till golden.

Sauce:

1 tsp. white wine vinegar
4 T. butter, melted
1 tsp. dry mustard
2 T. parsley
2 T. soy sauce

Whisk to mix well. Serve with pancakes. These are good as a side dish with meat or as a main dish for a light meal with salad.

Calories 470, protein 14.5 gm, sugars 3.25 gm, fiber 15.75 gm, sat. fat 5.5 gm, poly. fat 10.7 mg, choles. 101.25 mg, sodium 547.5 mg, potas. 590.7 mg. Analysis for $1/4$ recipe.

MAIN DISHES

PINTO CASSEROLE

2 c. pinto beans, cooked
1/2 c. bacon or cubed ham
1 lg. onion, chopped
1/4 tsp. garlic powder
1/2 tsp. pepper
1/2 tsp. oregano
1/4 tsp. cumin
3 tsp. chili powder
1 c. tomato sauce

Saute onion in a little oil. Add all but the beans with a cup of the bean liquid to the onion. Cook 10 minutes. Add mixture to beans. Cover and simmer 2 hours or put in oven-proof casserole and bake, covered, 2 hours at 325°. Serve with grated sharp cheese.

Calories 273, protein 15.8 gm, sugars 4.9 gm, fiber 21 gm, sat. fat .6 gm, poly. fat .19 mg, choles. 3 mg, sodium 230 mg, potas. 810.8 mg. Analysis for 1/8 recipe.

MAIN DISHES

PINTO BEAN CHALUPAS

1$1/2$ c. pinto beans
4 c. water
1 (4-oz.) can green chilies
1 lg. onion, chopped
$1/2$ tsp. oregano
1$1/2$ tsp. cumin
$1/2$ tsp. Italian seasoning
6 (6-inch) tortillas
1 lg. tomato, chopped
1 c. Monterey Jack cheese, shredded
Lettuce, shredded
2 T. black olives, sliced
$1/2$ c. plain yogurt

Soak and cook beans in the 4 cups water. Add next 5 ingredients. Bring to a boil and simmer 1$1/2$ hours. Puree 1 cup of the mixture and return to kettle. Simmer 30 minutes. Uncover and cook 20 minutes more or till beans are tender and mixture is thickened and liquid is absorbed. Stir often to prevent sticking. Heat tortillas; spread each with $1/2$ cup bean mixture. Serve on shredded lettuce. Sprinkle with tomato, cheese, olives and top with yogurt. Makes 6 servings.

Calories 390, protein 17.5 gm, sugars 55.3 gm, fiber 24.6 gm, sat. fat .9 gm, poly. fat .41 mg, choles. 2.66 mg, sodium 179 mg, potas. 1067 mg. Analysis for $1/6$ of recipe.

MAIN DISHES

CORNBREAD CHILI PIE

1 c. cooked kidney beans
1 med. onion, chopped
1 lb. hamburger, browned & drained
1 c. tomatoes
1 tsp. chili powder
1 tsp. Worcestershire sauce

Mix all together and simmer 15 minutes. Pour into a greased 9-inch square casserole. Top with cornbread batter. Bake at 425° for 20 minutes or till cornbread tests done.

Cornbread:

$1/2$ c. flour
$3/4$ c. yellow cornmeal
2 tsp. baking powder
1 egg
$1/2$ c. milk
2 T. salad oil

Mix all ingredients; stir just to moisten well. Serves 6.

Calories 435.4 , protein 20.8 gm, sugars 3.7 gm, fiber 5.8 gm, sat. fat 6.96 gm, poly. fat 3.4 mg, choles. 102.16 mg, sodium 92.7 mg, potas. 513 mg. Analysis for $1/6$ recipe.

Marriage is an institution held together by three books: Bible, Check and Cook.

RECIPE FOR FRIENDSHIP

Take some morning sunshine
Add a smile, some kind words too,
Sprinkle in some happy hours
It's not very hard to do.
Add a little thoughtfulness
Stir it just enough to blend
Serve it warm with loving hands
It's the makings of a friend.

BEAN BURGERS

2 c. cooked beans, mashed
2 eggs
1 lg. onion, chopped
1 c. whole-wheat flour
1 carrot, grated

Mix beans with eggs, onion and carrot. Add flour, a little at a time and mix well. Form into patties, $1/2$ inch thick and 3 inches in diameter. Fry in a little oil for 2-3 minutes on each side. Drain on paper towels. They are a little sticky before frying. Serve with catsup or salsa. Makes 12 patties.

Calories 91.7, protein 5 gm, sugars 1.7 gm, fiber 4.7 gm, sat. fat .275 gm, poly. fat .216 mg, choles. 33.75 mg, sodium 14.16 mg, potas. 192.16 mg. Analysis for 1 patty.

MAIN DISHES

HIGH PROTEIN MEAT LOAF

1 c. refried beans
1 egg, beaten
1/4 c. water
1 sm. onion, chopped
1 1/2 lbs. hamburger
1/4 c. cheddar cheese, grated
2 tsp. chili powder

Mix all ingredients well. Pat firmly into 5 1/2-cup ring mold. Turn mixture out into a greased, shallow baking dish. Bake at 350° for 35 minutes. Sprinkle with cheese and bake 5 minutes more or till cheese melts. Makes 6 servings.

Calories 403, protein 31.5 gm, sugars .5 gm, fiber 3.3 gm, sat. fat 9.9 gm, poly. fat 1.1 mg, choles. 138 mg, sodium 295 mg, potas. 509.3 mg. Analysis for 1/6 recipe.

FALAFEL

1/2 c. raw bulgur wheat
5 c. cooked & drained garbanzo beans
1/2 tsp. garlic powder
3 T. tahini
3 T. whole-wheat flour
2 T. soy sauce
1 tsp. cumin
1 tsp. coriander
1 tsp. turmeric
1/4 tsp. cayenne
1/3 c. water
4 T. fresh parsley, chopped or cilantro

Put bulgur in a bowl; pour 2 cups boiling water over it and let stand for 20 minutes. Meanwhile, combine remaining ingredients, except parsley in food processor or blender. Process until well mixed. Drain bulgur; mix with garbanzo mixture and parsley. Shape into patties. Cook by one of the following methods: **1.** Place on nonstick baking sheet and bake at 350° for 15 minutes. Turn over and bake another 15 minutes. **2.** Fry in oiled frying pan over medium heat, turning to cook each side. **Note:** Tahini is a nutritious, tasty paste of ground sesame seed, in its own oil, found in health food stores.

Calories 171.5, protein 8.5 gm, sugars .1 gm, sat. fat .55 gm, poly. fat 2 mg, choles. 0 mg, sodium 361.5 mg, potas. 281.3 mg. Analysis for 1/10 recipe.

MAIN DISHES

TOSTADA PIZZA

2 T. yellow cornmeal
2 c. packaged biscuit mix
1 lb. hamburger
3 T. green chilies
1 env. taco seasoning mix
2 c. refried beans
1 c. cheese, shredded
1 c. lettuce, shredded
1 tomato, chopped
1/2 c. onion, chopped
Taco sauce

Sprinkle a greased 12-inch pizza pan with cornmeal. Combine biscuit mix with 1/2 cup water. Stir with fork until well mixed. Turn out onto lightly floured surface and knead 6 times. Roll into a 14-inch circle and pat into prepared pan, crimping edges. Bake at 425° for 12 minutes or till golden. Meanwhile, brown meat; drain off fat. Add chilies, seasoning mix and 3/4 cup water. Bring to a boil; simmer, uncovered, for 10-15 minutes. Spread beans over crust and top with meat mixture. Bake at 425° for 8-10 minutes. Top with cheese and bake 2 minutes more. Garnish with tomato, lettuce, onion and taco sauce. Serves 6.

Calories 402, protein 13 gm, sugars 3.16 gm, fiber 9.3 gm, sat. fat 3.46 gm, poly. fat 5.8 mg, choles. 9 mg, sodium 496.6 mg, potas. 546.3 mg. Analysis for 1/6 recipe.

AUNT EVELYN'S BAKED BEANS

2 c. dried navy beans
1/2 lb. bacon
1 tsp. dry mustard
2 tsp. salt
1 onion
1/4 c. molasses

Wash beans. Soak by your favorite method. Put into a large pot; cover with water. Mix molasses, salt and mustard with a cup of the bean cooking water and pour over beans Poke the onion down into the pot. Place bacon over the top. Cover and bake at 300° for 5-6 hours, uncovering the last hour. If necessary, add more water during cooking. **Options: 1.** If you like a tomato flavor, add 1/4 cup chili sauce or catsup to the recipe or substitute tomato juice for the cooking water. **2.** Brown sugar may be used instead of molasses or use 1 cup of maple syrup. **3.** Beans may be cooked until tender. Then add other ingredients and bake 1 1/2 hours to get a full, rich flavor.

Calories 285, protein 19.38 gm, sugars 7.8 gm, fiber 14.5 gm, sat. fat 4.8 gm, poly. fat 1.5 mg, choles. 24 mg, sodium 1026 mg, potas. 689.6 mg. Analysis for 1/8 recipe.

Happiness often sneaks in through a door you didn't know you left open.

MAIN DISHES

HAWAIIAN BAKED BEANS

2 c. Great Northern beans, cooked & drained
$1/2$ c. onion, chopped
$1/4$ c. salad oil
$1/8$ tsp. garlic powder
$1/4$ c. dark brown sugar
1 (15-oz.) can tomato sauce
$1/4$ c. molasses
$1/4$ tsp. pepper
1 (12-oz.) can pineapple chunks, drained

Saute onion in salad oil. Mix in garlic powder, sugar, tomato sauce, molasses and pepper. Simmer 20 minutes. Mix in beans and pineapple. Put in 3-quart greased casserole; cover. Bake 1 hour at 350°. Uncover and bake 15 minutes more. Add pineapple liquid, if needed. **Option:** Bacon or salt pork may be added.

Calories 365.6, protein 15.25 gm, sugars 21.37 gm, fiber 20.6 gm, sat. fat .875 gm, poly. fat 4 mg, choles. 0 mg, sodium 334 mg, potas. 951.5 mg. Analysis for $1/8$ recipe.

BLACK BEAN CORNBREAD CASSEROLE

2 c. black beans, cooked & drained
1 lb. pork sausage
1 c. onion, chopped
1 c. celery, chopped
2 c. whole-kernel corn, drained
3 c. fresh mushrooms, chopped
1/2 c. parsley
1/4 c. margarine, melted
1/4 tsp. pepper
1 tsp. sage
5 c. cornbread, coarsely crumbled
3/4 c. chicken broth

In a large skillet, cook sausage, onion and celery until sausage is brown; drain. In a large bowl, mix next 6 ingredients. Gently stir in cornbread. Mix in enough broth to moisten. Bake in greased, uncovered, 4-quart casserole at 375° for 45 minutes or till heated through.

Calories 478, protein 18.37 gm, sugars 8.5 gm, fiber 9.75 gm, sat. fat 8.2 gm, poly. fat 4.26 mg. choles. 72.6 mg, sodium 1131.8 mg, potas. 665 mg. Analysis for 1/8 recipe.

MAIN DISHES

BLACK BEANS WITH NO-COOK SALSA

1¹/₂ c. black beans, cooked & drained

Salsa:

6 med. tomatoes, peeled & chopped
2 T. onion, chopped
¹/₄ tsp. garlic powder
2 tsp. basil
1 tsp. thyme

Combine all ingredients. Let stand 30 minutes to meld flavors. Add salt to taste, at serving time. (It will draw out moisture from tomatoes, making salsa too watery, if added earlier.) Top hot corn tortillas with black beans, sliced avocado and sour cream.

CHALUPA

2 c. pinto beans, soaked
3 lbs. pork roast
7 c. water
1 med. onion, chopped
1/4 tsp. garlic powder
2 tsp. cumin
2 T. chili powder
1 tsp. oregano
1 (4-oz.) can green chilies

Put all ingredients in a large, heavy pan. Cover and simmer 5 hours or till roast and beans are tender. Uncover and cook 1/2 hour to thicken. Remove meat and cut into bite-sized pieces. Return to pan and reheat. Serve with tortilla chips, chopped tomato, lettuce, onion, grated cheese and salsa.

Calories 702.5, protein 60 gm, sugars 3.37 gm, fiber 20.75 gm, sat. fat 10.7 gm, poly. fat 3.5 mg, choles. 162 mg, sodium 100 mg, potas. 1382.8 mg. Analysis for 1/8 recipe.

SOYBEAN CASSEROLE

1¹/₂ c. dry soybeans, washed & soaked

Bring beans to a boil in 4 cups water. Cover and simmer 2 hours or until tender. Drain.

1 c. onion, chopped
2 T. salad oil
¹/₄ c. flour
¹/₄ tsp. savory
¹/₄ tsp. thyme
¹/₄ tsp. sage
1 c. sharp cheese, grated
¹/₂ c. bread crumbs

In a saucepan, heat oil; stir in flour. Add 1¹/₂ cups water and herbs. Cook and stir till bubbly. Stir in soybeans. Put in greased 1¹/₂-quart casserole. Bake, uncovered, at 350° for 15 minutes. Mix cheese with crumbs; sprinkle on top of beans. Bake 15 minutes more. Makes 6-8 servings.

Calories 431.6, protein 28 gm, sugars 2.16 gm, fiber .83 gm, sat. fat 4.2 gm, poly. fat 10 mg, choles. 9.3 mg, sodium 115 mg, potas. 817 mg. Analysis for ¹/₆ recipe.

MAIN DISHES

BAKED LENTILS & CHEESE

1³/₄ c. lentils, rinsed
2¹/₂ qts. water
1 bay leaf

Simmer 30 minutes or till tender. Drain and remove bay leaf. Put lentils in a greased 9 x 13-inch pan. Mix the following ingredients and put on top of lentils.

2 c. onion, chopped
¹/₂ tsp. garlic powder
1 c. carrots, sliced
¹/₂ c. celery, sliced
¹/₂ c. green pepper, chopped
1 (16-oz.) can tomatoes, drained
¹/₂ tsp. pepper
¹/₄ tsp. marjoram
¹/₄ tsp. sage
¹/₄ tsp. thyme
1 c. American cheese, chopped

Cover and bake at 375° for 1 hour and 15 minutes. Serves 8.

Calories 126, protein 8.25 gm, sugars 4.87 gm, fiber 4.5 gm, sat. fat 1.28 gm, poly. fat .2 mg, choles. 6.75 mg, sodium 60 mg, potas. 467.75 mg. Analysis for ¹/₈ recipe.

MAIN DISHES

TOSTADAS

1¹/₂ c. refried beans
2 T. chili powder
1 T. cumin
1¹/₂ c. fresh salsa
6 tortillas
2 c. chicken, diced
1 c. Monterey Jack cheese, grated
3 c. lettuce, shredded
1 avocado, sliced
Sour cream

Mix spices into beans; heat till hot. Heat sauce just till hot. Heat tortillas, just till hot and spread each with ¹/₄ cup beans, 2 tablespoons sauce, ¹/₃ cup chicken and 2 tablespoons more sauce. Sprinkle with cheese. Broil 3 inches from heat, about 3 minutes, till cheese melts. Top with lettuce, avocados and sour cream.

Calories 465, protein 27 gm, sugars 15.8 gm, fiber 8.5 gm, sat. fat 5.75 gm, poly. fat 2.35 mg, choles. 62.8 mg, sodium 1460 mg, potas. 1037.5 mg. Analysis for ¹/₆ recipe, sour cream not included.

Music is the way our memories sing to us across time.

VEGETARIAN CASSEROLE

1 c. black beans, cooked & drained
1 c. lentils, cooked & drained
1$^1/_2$ c. spaghetti sauce
2 T. salad oil
4 lg. green peppers, cut into $^1/_4$ inch strips
$^1/_2$ tsp. garlic powder
1 c. Parmesan cheese, grated
1$^1/_2$ c. Monterey Jack cheese, shredded

In a large skillet, saute peppers in salad oil till tender. Puree lentils and spaghetti sauce. In large bowl, combine lentil mixture, black beans, garlic powder, peppers and $^1/_2$ cup Parmesan cheese; mix well. Place in shallow 2$^1/_2$-quart greased casserole dish. Sprinkle top with Monterey Jack cheese and remaining Parmesan. Bake at 350° for 35 minutes or till golden and bubbly. Makes 8-10 servings.

Calories 420, protein 16 gm, sugars 5.37 gm, fiber 11.5 gm, sat. fat 4.7 gm, poly. fat 3.6 mg, choles. 16.87 mg, sodium 695 mg, potas. 810.8 mg. Analysis for $^1/_8$ recipe.

MAIN DISHES

ANASAZI BAKED BEANS

2 c. anasazi beans, washed
2 c. orange juice
2 c. water
1 (8-oz.) can tomato sauce
1 med. onion, chopped
1/4 c. molasses
2 T. Worcestershire sauce
1/4 lb. bacon, cut up

Mix all ingredients in a greased 3-quart casserole. Bake, covered, in 300° oven 3 hours or till beans are softened, but not mushy. Increase heat to 325°. Uncover, stir and bake 30 minutes more, until beans are tender and sauce is thickened.

Calories 441, protein 24.5 gm, sugars 13.88 gm, fiber 23.1 gm, sat. fat 5 gm, poly. fat 1.975 mg, choles. 24 mg, sodium 617.5 mg, potas. 1090.75. Analysis for 1/8 recipe.

DIPS & SALADS

PINTO BEAN DIP

1 c. cooked pintos, mashed
$1/4$ c. celery, diced
$1/4$ c. walnuts, chopped
2 T. mayonnaise
2 T. red onion
$1/4$ tsp. garlic salt

Mix all ingredients well. Add salt and pepper to taste.

CHEESY BEAN DIP

$2^1/2$ c. refried beans
1 c. cheddar cheese, shredded
$1/2$ c. green onions, chopped
2 T. taco sauce

Mix in medium saucepan. Simmer, stirring often for 30 minutes. Serve hot with tortilla chips.

BLACK BEAN DIP

1 c. black beans, cooked
2 T. salad oil
1 med. onion, chopped
1 tsp. garlic powder
$1/2$ tsp. pepper
2 T. Worcestershire sauce
$1/2$ c. milk
1 (4-oz.) can green chilies
$1/2$ tsp. hot sauce

Fry onion till brown. Add rest of ingredients. Put in blender and puree. Return to pan and simmer on LOW heat 20 minutes. Stir to prevent burning. Serve hot or cold with chips, crackers or tortillas. Makes $1^1/2$ cups. **Option:** May be frozen and reheated in microwave.

DIPS & SALADS

PARTY TIME DIP

4 c. refried beans
1 (4-oz.) can green chilies
1/2 c. sour cream
1/2 c. mayonnaise
2 T. lemon juice
2 avocados, chopped
1/2 c. picante sauce
1 c. cheddar cheese, grated
1 c. Monterey Jack cheese, grated
4 green onions, chopped
1/2 c. black olives, chopped

Spread beans in greased 9 x 13-inch pan. Mix sour cream and mayonnaise; spread over beans. Sprinkle lemon juice over avocados; layer over cream mixture. Pour picante sauce over top. Sprinkle cheeses, onions and olives on top of sauce. this may be served cold or baked at 350°, uncovered, for 30 minutes. Serve with tortilla chips.

BEAN DIP

1 c. cooked pintos, mashed
1 (4-oz.) can green chilies
1 T. onion, chopped
1/2 c. cheddar cheese, grated
1 sm. tomato, chopped
1/8 tsp. hot sauce

Mix all ingredients in pan. Heat over low heat, stirring till cheese melts. Serve hot with tortilla chips.

A day of worry is more exhausting than a week of work.

SANDWICH SPREAD

3½ c. cooked pintos, drained
2 c. cottage cheese
1/2 c. sweet pickle relish
1 c. bacon, cooked & crumbled
1/4 c. onion, chopped
1 T. prepared mustard
2 T. picante sauce

Mix all ingredients in blender till smooth. Chill several hours. Use for sandwiches or a dip with chips.

BLACK BEAN & TOFU SALAD

1 c. black beans
4 c. water
1 c. tofu, cut into 1/2-inch cubes
1 c. whole-kernel corn
1 c. sweet red pepper, chopped
1/2 c. scallions, chopped
2 oz. white miso
4 oz. rice vinegar
1 tsp. dried red pepper flakes

Cook beans in 4 cups water 1 hour or till beans are just tender. Drain and rinse with cold water to cool. Mix tofu, corn, pepper, scallions and beans. Whisk miso, vinegar and pepper flakes together and toss with bean mixture. Makes 6 servings.

Calories 183, protein 13.6 gm, sugars 1.3 gm, fiber 8.6 gm, sat. fat .7 gm, poly. fat 2.6 mg, choles. 0 mg, sodium 519.2 mg, potas. 418.8 mg. Analysis for 1/6 recipe.

YUMMY BLACK BEAN SALAD

1 c. black beans, cooked till just tender
1 med. apple, diced
1 ripe papaya, diced

Dressing:

3 green onions, chopped
1/4 tsp. garlic powder
1/4 tsp. cumin
3 T. lemon juice
1/3 c. orange juice
2 T. salad oil
1 tsp. pepper
1/2 tsp. cinnamon
2 T. cider vinegar

Stir together all ingredients. Toss apple with dressing to prevent discoloration. Mix beans with papaya and combine with dressing. Chill at least 20 minutes before serving. This can be made a day ahead. Serves 6.

Calories 160, protein 5.7 gm, sugars 9.5 gm, fiber 8.7 gm, sat. fat .7 gm, poly. fat 2.86 mg, choles. 0 mg, sodium 2.5 mg, potas. 408.6 mg. Analysis for 1/6 recipe.

LAYERED BLACK BEAN SALAD

1½ c. cooked black beans
1 c. lettuce, shredded
¼ c. green pepper
½ c. whole-kernel corn, cooked
1 avocado, sliced

Layer in large bowl: ³/₄ cup beans, lettuce, pepper, corn, ³/₄ cup beans, avocado.

Dressing:

2 T. lime juice
1 T. cilantro
⅛ tsp. garlic powder
½ c. olive oil

Mix in blender until thick, pouring oil in gradually.

Protein 5.3 gm, sugars 2 gm, fiber 7.3 gm, sat. fat 3 gm, poly. fat 2.8 mg, choles. 0 mg, sodium 53.3 mg, potas. 482.8 mg. Analysis for ¹/₆ recipe.

BLACK BEAN & CORN SALAD

1¹/₂ c. black beans, cooked & drained
4 Anaheim peppers
2 tsp. cumin
¹/₄ c. wine vinegar
1 T. Dijon style mustard
2 tsp. pepper
¹/₂ c. olive oil
2 c. whole-kernel corn, drained
18 cherry tomatoes, halved
3 scallions, sliced

Roast peppers under broiler until skins are slightly charred. Seal in paper bag to steam for 10 minutes. Rub away charred skin and cut into ¹/₂-inch pieces. In a small bowl, whisk together the spices, mustard and oil. In a large bowl, mix beans, peppers and corn. Pour dressing over salad. This can be done to this point up to 24 hours ahead. Cover and refrigerate. Return to room temperature before proceeding. Add tomatoes and scallions. Toss well. Season with salt to taste. Best served at room temperature. This is very good with grilled meat.

Calories 294, protein 11.87 gm, sugars 5.5 gm, fiber 17 gm, sat. fat 1.58 gm, poly. fat 1.6 mg, choles. 0 mg, sodium 176.25 mg, potas. 733.6 mg. Analysis for ¹/₈ recipe.

PINTO & POTATO SALAD

2 c. potatoes, cooked & diced
2 c. cooked pintos, drained
$\frac{1}{2}$ c. mayonnaise
1 c. plain yogurt
1 c. cucumber, peeled & chopped
1 sm. onion, chopped
Salt & pepper to taste

Mix mayonnaise, yogurt, cucumber, onion, salt and pepper. Mix with potatoes and beans until well combined. Cover and chill till serving time. **Option:** Use pink beans.

Calories 198, protein 8 gm, sugars 4.7 gm, fiber 7.8 gm, sat. fat .95 gm, poly. fat 1.98 mg, choles. 6.3 mg, sodium 120 mg, potas. 559.3 mg. Analysis for $\frac{1}{6}$ recipe.

Children have never been good at listening to their elders, but they never fail to imitate them.

CALICO SALAD

1 pkg. Mitie Mixes Calico soup mix
1 med. onion, chopped
1 green pepper, chopped
1/2 c. salad oil
1/2 c. vinegar
1/2 c. sugar
1/4 tsp. pepper

(**Option:** Omit sugar; add 1/2 teaspoon oregano, 1/2 teaspoon garlic powder and artificial sweetener to taste.) Wash and soak soup mix. Put in a large pot with 5 cups water. Bring to a boil; cook 1 1/2 hours or till tender. Drain. Stir in remaining ingredients. Chill. Best if marinated overnight.

Calories 389, protein 12.16 gm, sugars 19.8 gm, sat. fat 1.75 gm, poly. fat 8.1 mg, choles. 0 mg, sodium 1.67 mg, potas. 596.8 mg. Analysis for 1/6 recipe.

TACO SALAD

1 can kidney beans, drained
1 lb. hamburger, browned & drained
1 onion, chopped
1 head lettuce, chopped
2 tomatoes, chopped
1 lb. Monterey Jack cheese, grated
1 pkg. tortilla chips, broken
1 (8-oz.) bottle Russian dressing

Mix all but chips and dressing; chill. At serving time, mix dressing and chips with salad.

Calories 1022, protein 31 gm, sugars 4.8 gm, fiber 11.67 gm, sat. fat 15.26 gm, poly. fat 10.13 mg, choles. 98 mg, sodium 938.5 mg, potas. 868.5 mg. Analysis for $1/6$ recipe.

THREE BEAN SALAD

2 limes
$3/4$ c. thick & chunky salsa
$1/3$ c. salad oil
$1^1/2$ tsp. chili powder
2 c. cooked black beans, drained
2 c. cooked kidney beans, drained
2 c. cooked garbanzo beans, drained
2 stalks celery, sliced
1 med. red onion, sliced
1 med. tomato, diced

1 hour before serving or early in the day: In a large bowl, squeeze lime juice; stir in salsa, salad oil and chili powder. Add beans, celery, onions and tomato. Toss to mix. Serve at room temperature or cover and chill to serve later. Makes 10 servings.

GELATIN & PINTO BEAN SALAD

1 (3-oz.) pkg. lime gelatin
3 T. vinegar
1 T. onion, minced
1 c. green pepper, chopped
2 c. cooked pinto beans, drained

Prepare gelatin as directed on package, using vinegar as part of liquid. Set aside to cool. Put 1/2 of beans in 8-inch cake pan. Sprinkle onion and green peppers over beans. Top with rest of beans. Pour cooled gelatin over top. Chill till firm. Serve over lettuce.

BLACK BEAN RELISH

2 c. cooked black beans, drained
3/4 c. tomato, chopped
1 T. jalapeno
1/2 c. sweet red pepper
1/4 c. red onion
2 T. white vinegar
1 T. salad oil

Mix well. Cover and chill 1 hour. Serve with salads, tortillas, chicken or fish.

FRESH TOMATO SALSA

6 med. tomatoes, peeled & chopped
2 T. green onion, finely chopped
$1/8$ tsp. garlic powder
1 tsp. basil
1 tsp. thyme
$1/4$ tsp. pepper
Salt to taste just before serving

Mix all ingredients. Let salsa stand at least 30 minutes. Serve over corn tortillas, topped with black beans, avocado slices and sour cream. Also good with linguine, fish or chicken.

DIPS & SALADS

Recipe Favorites

YELLOW SPLIT PEA SOUP

1 T. salad oil
1 T. butter
1 onion, chopped
1 stalk celery, chopped
6 c. chicken broth
2 c. yellow split peas
1 tsp. pepper
1 tsp. cumin
2 T. lemon juice

Saute onion in oil and butter, till golden. Add celery; cook till tender. Add broth and peas. Bring to a boil. Reduce heat and simmer, covered, for 1-1½ hours or till peas are very soft. Add spices. Puree till smooth. Return to pan and reheat. This will make a thick soup. Add water, if needed.

Calories 183, protein 12 gm, sugars .67 gm, fiber 4.17 gm, sat. fat 1.85 gm, poly. fat 1.5 mg, choles. 5.7 mg, sodium 788.3 mg, potas. 546.8 mg. Analysis for 1/6 recipe.

SOUPS

TASTY LIMA SOUP

1/2 lb. salt pork, diced or 1 hamhock
2 onions, chopped
2 stalks celery, chopped
2 carrots, chopped
1 tsp. garlic powder
2 c. baby lima beans
1/2 c. parsley
1 tsp. caraway seeds
1/2 tsp. hot sauce
2 T. white wine vinegar
1 c. milk

In large pan, cook salt pork 10 minutes or till golden. Add onions, celery and carrots; cook till vegetables are tender. Add garlic, limas, parsley, caraway, hot sauce and 6 cups water. Bring to a boil; heat and simmer 1 hour. If using hamhock, remove; cut meat off and return to soup. Puree soup. Return to pan; add vinegar and milk. Heat, but do not boil. Top each serving with chopped fresh dill, if desired.

Calories 467, protein 31.3 gm, sugars 5.3 gm, fiber 32 gm, sat. fat 3.86 gm, poly. fat 1.18 mg, choles. 49.3 mg, sodium 383.3 mg, potas. 1603 mg. Analysis for 1/6 recipe.

SOUPS

CALICO SOUP

1 pkg. Mitie Mixes Calico soup mix
6 c. water
1 hamhock
1 lg. onion, chopped
1 (16-oz.) can tomatoes
2 tsp. chili powder
3 T. lemon juice

Wash and soak beans. Cook with 6 cups water and hamhock 1½ hours. Add the rest of the ingredients and simmer 30 minutes more or till beans are tender. Makes 2½ quarts. Leftovers freeze well. **Crockpot Option:** Cook 6-8 hours.

Calories 318, protein 15.1 gm, sugars 4.37 gm, fiber 13.5 gm, sat. fat 3.93 gm, poly. fat .987 mg, choles. 19.75 mg, sodium 279.37 mg, potas. 659 mg. Analysis for ⅛ recipe.

LIFE'S LITTLE PLEASURES
A pat on the back
A hug
A full moon
An empty parking space
A crackling fire
A glorious sunset
A great meal
Hot soup by Mitie Mixes

SOUPS

FIESTA SOUP

1 pkg. Mitie Mixes Fiesta Supreme soup mix
6 c. water
1 (16-oz.) can tomatoes
1 onion, chopped
1/8 tsp. garlic powder
1/2 jalapeno or 1 (4-oz.) can green chilies

Wash and soak beans. Cook beans with 6 cups water for 1 1/2 hours. Add rest of ingredients and cook 30 minutes more or till beans are tender. Makes 2 1/2 quarts. **Options:** This is great as a vegetarian soup or with ham, chicken, cooked sausage, soup bones. Salsa may be added.

Calories 158, protein 10.12 gm, sugars 3.6 gm, fiber 14.37 gm, sat. fat 0 gm, poly fat .137 mg, choles. 0 mg, sodium 0 mg, potas. 645 mg. Analysis for 1/8 recipe.

SPICY BLACK BEAN SOUP

1¹/₂ c. black beans
4 med. onions, chopped
1 green pepper, chopped
1 tsp. garlic powder
1 tsp. cumin
1 tsp. oregano
1 bay leaf
1 tsp. dry mustard
1 c. tomato, chopped
3 T. lemon juice
6 c. water

Wash beans. Mix all ingredients in a large pot. Cook 3 hours on top of stove or 6-8 hours in a crockpot.

Calories 242.5, protein 13.3 gm, sugars 2.66 gm, fiber 19.66 gm, sat. fat .18 gm, poly. fat .36 mg, choles. 0 mg, sodium 5 mg, potas. 657.8 mg. Analysis for ¹/₆ recipe.

COWBOY BEANS

2 c. pinto beans
2 T. sugar
1 (4-oz.) can green chilies
1/2 tsp. garlic powder
1 med. onion, chopped
1 T. Worcestershire sauce
1/2 lb. bacon, fried & diced

Soak pintos; cook in 6 cups water for 30 minutes. Add sugar, chilies, garlic and onions. Cook 3 hours or till beans are tender. Add Worcestershire and bacon. Makes 6 servings.

Calories 389, protein 21.16 gm, sugars 3.83 gm, fiber 30.3 gm, sat. fat 1.9 gm, poly. fat .8 mg, choles. 8 mg, sodium 171.6 mg, potas. 1262.5 mg. Analysis for 1/6 recipe.

VEGETARIAN CHILI

2 c. cooked kidney beans
2 c. cooked pinto beans
1 lg. onion, chopped
1 lg. green pepper, chopped
1 lg. carrot, chopped
1 tsp. garlic powder
2 1/2 c. boiling water
1 beef bouillon cube
1 c. tomato juice
1 (8-oz.) can tomato sauce
3 T. chili powder
1 (4-oz.) can green chilies
3/4 tsp. cumin
3/4 tsp. oregano
1/2 tsp. cinnamon
1 bay leaf
1/8 tsp. hot sauce

Put beans in large kettle, barely cover with water; bring to a boil. Mix boiling water with bouillon; add to beans with rest of ingredients. Simmer, uncovered, 45 minutes. Top each serving with 3 tablespoons shredded cheddar cheese and 1 tablespoon plain yogurt. Serves 6.

Calories 367, protein 21.16 gm, sugars 11.5 gm, fiber 30.8 gm, sat. fat 0 gm, poly. fat .21 mg, choles. 0 mg, sodium 40 mg, potas. 1393.8 mg. Analysis for 1/6 of recipe.

SOUPS

GREAT NORTHERN SOUP

2 c. Great Northern beans
1 hamhock
8 c. water
2 c. celery, chopped
1 onion, chopped
1 potato, chopped
1 (16-oz.) can tomatoes
2 tsp. parsley, chopped

Soak beans. Cook 1 1/2 hours; add hamhock and cook 2 hours more or till beans are tender. Add celery, onions and potatoes. Cook 20 minutes more or till tender. Add tomatoes and parsley. Heat through.

Calories 380, protein 24.5 gm, sugars 4.6 gm, fiber 20.6 gm, sat. fat 3.3 gm, poly. fat .82 mg, choles. 37.5 mg, sodium 345 mg, potas. 1031.7 mg. Analysis for 1/8 recipe.

MEATLESS CHILI

1 lb. red or kidney beans, soaked & cooked 1 hour, just till tender.

Add:

6 tomatoes, chopped
1/2 tsp. garlic powder
1 tsp. chili powder
1 green pepper, chopped
2 stalks celery, chopped
1 tsp. oregano
Salt to taste

Cook 1 hour or till veggies are tender. Top with grated cheese or sour cream. Serves 6.

Calories 186.6, protein 20.6 gm, sugars 9.8 gm, fiber 29 gm, sat. fat 0 gm, poly. fat .21 mg, choles. 0 mg, sodium 38 gm, potas. 1389 mg. Analysis for 1/6 of recipe.

WESTERN BLACK BEAN SOUP

1$1/2$ c. black beans
1 c. onion, chopped
1 tsp. garlic powder
2 T. salad oil
2 c. ham, cooked
6 c. chicken broth
1 T. pickled jalapeno
2 T. chili powder
2 T. cilantro
1 T. oregano
2 tsp. cumin

Put black beans in large kettle; cover with water. Bring to a boil. Let stand 1 hour. Cook onion and garlic in oil 6 minutes. Add with rest of ingredients to beans. Simmer 3 hours or till tender. Puree in blender. Serve with sour cream.

Calories 396, protein 27 gm, sugars .75 gm, fiber 17 gm, sat. fat 5.27 gm, poly. fat 3.43 mg, choles. 49.75 mg, sodium 994 mg, potas. 785.8 mg. Analysis for $1/8$ of recipe.

LENTIL & WALNUT SOUP

2 c. lentils, sorted & washed
5 T. olive oil
1 T. butter
1 lg. onion, sliced
$1/2$ c. parsley, chopped
$1/4$ lb. bacon or ham, cooked
$1/4$ tsp. pepper

Simmer $1^{1}/_{2}$ hours.

2 egg yolks
1 tsp. olive oil
1 T. vinegar

Mix with a little of the hot soup and stir into soup. Add $1/2$ cup finely chopped walnuts. Cook 20 minutes more. Stir often.

Calories 464, protein 26 gm, sugars .62 gm, fiber 9.25 gm, sat. fat 5.5 gm, poly. fat 2.2 mg, choles. 84.3 mg, sodium 277.5 mg, potas. 830.8 mg. Analysis for $1/8$ of recipe.

4-ALARM CHILI

1 lb. bulk Italian sausage
1 lg. onion, chopped
1$^1/_2$ tsp. garlic powder
2 c. pintos or kidney beans, cooked
2 (15-oz.) cans tomato sauce
1 (24-oz.) can tomatoes, chopped
1 beef bouillon cube
1 c. water
2 T. chili powder
1 tsp. cinnamon
2 T. green chilies, chopped
Cheddar cheese, shredded
Plain yogurt

In large kettle, cook sausage and onion till browned; drain. Add next 9 ingredients. Simmer, uncovered, for 45 minutes. Top each serving with cheese and a dollop of yogurt. Makes 6 servings.

Calories 475, protein 23 gm, sugars 14.6 gm, fiber 11.5 gm, sat. fat 10.3 gm, poly. fat 2.2 mg, choles. 59.3 mg, sodium 1743.3 mg, potas. 1359.3 mg. Analysis for $^1/_6$ of recipe.

BLACK BEAN CHILI

1^1/$_2$ c. black beans
1 onion, chopped
^{1}/$_2$ c. tomato, chopped
2^1/$_4$ tsp. cumin
2^1/$_4$ tsp. oregano
1^1/$_2$ tsp. paprika
^{1}/$_4$ tsp. cayenne pepper
1^1/$_2$ tsp. chili powder
2 cloves garlic, minced
4 tsp. canned green chilies
1 bay leaf

Wash black beans. Heat ^{1}/$_4$ cup salad oil in a large pot. Saute onion. Add remaining ingredients and beans with 4 cups water. Bring to a boil. Simmer 2^1/$_2$ hours or till tender. Before serving, put ^{1}/$_2$ cup grated Monterey Jack cheese into each bowl. Pour chili into bowls and top with sour cream. Makes 5 cups.

Calories 281, protein 18.8 gm, sugars 2.8 gm, fiber 28.2 gm, sat. fat .26 gm, poly. fat .6 mg, choles. 0 mg, sodium 6 mg, potas. 909.4 mg. Analysis for ^{1}/$_5$ of recipe.

The way to a man's heart is through his stomach-......keep it healthy with lots of good home cooking.

SOUPS

BEAN & VEGGIE SOUP

2 c. Great Northern beans
8 c. water
1 meaty hambone
1 c. celery, chopped
1 c. carrot, chopped
1 med. potato, peeled & chopped
1 bay leaf
$1/4$ tsp. pepper

Wash and soak beans. Combine beans, water and hambone in a large pot. Bring to a boil cover and simmer 2 hours or till beans are just soft. Add rest of ingredients. Cook 1 hour more or till beans are very tender. Cut meat from hambone and return it to soup. Puree 2 cups of soup in the blender; return to pan and reheat.

Calories 437.5, protein 28.37 gm, sugars 3.25 gm, fiber 20.25 gm, sat. fat 5 gm, poly. fat 1.26 mg, choles. 56.25 mg, sodium 505 mg, potas. 946.8 mg. Analysis for $1/8$ of recipe.

BLACK BEAN VEGGIE SOUP

1$1/2$ c. black beans
3 c. water
$3/4$ c. celery, chopped
$3/4$ c. onion, chopped
$1/2$ c. carrot, chopped
6 c. beef broth
1 hamhock
$1/2$ tsp. oregano
1 tsp. pepper
2 tsp. garlic
$1/4$ tsp. cloves
1 bay leaf

Wash beans. Simmer above ingredients in a large kettle 2 hours. Add 1 (8-ounce) can tomato sauce and $1/2$ cup uncooked rice. Cook another $1/2$ hour or till beans are tender. Cut meat off bone. Makes 2$1/2$ quarts.

Calories 300.6, protein 20.87 gm, sugars 1.12 gm, fiber 17.5 gm, sat. fat 3.5 gm, poly. fat 1.16 mg, choles. 37.5 mg, sodium 643 mg, potas. 707.8 mg. Analysis for $1/8$ of recipe.

BARBECUED BEAN SOUP

2¹/₂ c. pinto beans
8 c. water
2 c. carrots, chopped
1 c. onion, chopped
1 meaty hambone
1 (16-oz.) can tomatoes
¹/₄ c. vinegar
2 T. brown sugar
2 T. Worcestershire sauce
2 tsp. prepared mustard

Wash and soak beans. Cook with water, carrots, onion and hambone for 2¹/₂ hours. Add the rest of ingredients and cook ¹/₂ hour more or till beans are tender. Remove hambone; cut meat off of it and return meat to soup. Mash some of the beans in the blender to help thicken soup. Makes 8-10 servings.

Calories 422.5, protein 24 gm, sugars 10.6 gm, fiber 24.37 gm, sat. fat 3.56 gm, poly. fat 1.1, choles. 37.5 mg, sodium 384.37 mg, potas. 1177 mg. Analysis for ¹/₈ of recipe.

BEAN & SQUASH SOUP

2$^1/_2$ c. Great Northern beans
8 c. water
4 c. winter squash, pared & cubed
1 meaty hambone
1 c. onion, chopped
1 c. celery, chopped
$^1/_4$ tsp. pepper

Wash and soak beans. Mix all ingredients. Bring to a boil; cover and simmer 2 hours or till beans are tender. Remove meat form hambone. Return meat to soup. Mash some of the beans to thicken soup. Simmer till it heated through. Makes 8-10 servings.

Calories 362.5, protein 23.8 gm, sugars 3.6 gm, fiber 20.5 gm, sat. fat 3.3 gm, poly. fat .825 mg, choles. 37.5 mg, sodium 332.5 mg. potas. 876.6 mg. Analysis for $^1/_8$ of recipe.

SOUPS

LENTIL HAM SOUP

1¹/₂ c. lentils, washed
5 c. water
2 T. salad oil
¹/₂ c. celery, chopped
1 med. onion, chopped
¹/₄ tsp. garlic powder
1 meaty hambone
1 (16-oz.) can tomatoes

Saute celery and onion in oil in large pot. Add remaining ingredients. Bring to a boil; simmer 2 hours or till lentils are tender. Remove meat from bone; return it to soup. Makes 8 servings.

Calories 348, protein 22.8 gm, sugars 2.37 gm, fiber 7.5 gm, sat. fat 3.7 mg, poly. fat 3.17 mg, choles. 37.5 mg, sodium 326.2 mg, potas. 795 mg. Analysis for ¹/₈ of recipe.

SOUPS

VEGETARIAN LENTIL SOUP

2 c. lentils, washed
2¹/₂ qts. water
1 c. barley
¹/₂ c. salad oil
1 c. onion, chopped
1 c. celery with leaves, chopped
1 lg. potato, diced
3 T. parsley
¹/₄ tsp. pepper
1 (16-oz.) can tomatoes

Place all ingredients in a large pot. Bring to a boil; cover and simmer 1 hour or till lentils are tender. Stir occasionally. Add more water, if needed. Makes about 4 quarts.

Calories 404, protein 17.25 gm, sugars 3.87 gm, fiber 10 gm, sat. fat 1.31 gm, poly. fat 6.4 mg, choles. 0 mg, sodium 12.5 mg, potas. 891 mg. Analysis for ¹/₈ of recipe.

SOUPS

BEST EVER NAVY BEAN SOUP

4 c. Navy beans, washed & soaked
1¹/₂ lbs. hamhocks
4 qts. water
1 lg. onion, chopped

Put beans, hamhocks and water in a large pot. Bring to a boil; cover and simmer 3 hours. Saute onion in a little margarine. When light brown, add to soup. Remove meat from bone; return to soup. Puree 2 cups of the beans and return to soup. Reheat. When ready to serve, season with salt and pepper. **Option:** Use Great Northern Beans.

SOYBEAN CHILI

1 lb. hamburger
1/2 c. water
4 c. cooked soybeans
2 qts. tomatoes
1 1/2 c. onion, chopped
1/2 tsp. garlic powder
4 tsp. chili powder
1 tsp. cumin
2 cans kidney beans, undrained

Brown hamburger; stir in rest of ingredients, except kidney beans. Cover, cook 2 hours; stir in kidney beans. Cook 1/2 hour more. Serve over hot rice. Makes 2 1/2 quarts.

Calories 421, protein 34.3 gm, sugars 8.5 gm, fiber 7.8 gm, sat. fat 5.58 gm, poly. fat 4.7 mg, choles. 50.6 mg, sodium 46.3 mg, potas. 1300 mg. Analysis for 1/8 of recipe.

SOUPS

MINESTRONE

1 onion, chopped
1¹/₂ c. celery, chopped
1 (24-oz.) can tomatoes
1 (6-oz.) can tomato paste
3 c. water
¹/₂ c. parsley, chopped
1 bay leaf
1 tsp. oregano
2 tsp. basil
¹/₄ tsp. garlic powder
2 c. chopped carrot, zucchini, potato, green beans, corn, cabbage or whatever veggies you have on hand
¹/₂ c. pearled barley
¹/₂ c. spaghetti, broken
1 c. cooked black or pinto beans

Mix all but spaghetti and cooked beans in a large soup pan. Simmer 1 hour or till veggies are almost tender. Add spaghetti and cooked beans; cook 30 minutes more. Add salt and pepper to taste.

Calories 131.8, protein 5.5 gm, sugars 8.25 gm, fiber 6.75 gm, sat. fat .06 gm, poly. fat .175 mg, choles. 0 mg, sodium 56.2 mg, potas. 632.8 mg. Analysis for ¹/₈ of recipe.

BLACK BEAN SOUP

1¹/₂ c. black beans
1 T. salad oil
1 lg. onion, diced
1 lg. green pepper, diced
2 tsp. garlic powder
1 (15-oz.) can tomato sauce
2 tsp. salt
¹/₂ tsp. pepper

In a large kettle, over high heat, cook washed beans with 8 cups water. Bring to a boil. Cover and let stand 1 hour. In large skillet, heat oil, onion and pepper. Stir till tender. Stir into undrained beans. Add garlic powder, tomato sauce, salt and pepper. Cover and simmer 2 hours or till tender. Stir occasionally. Makes 9 (1 cup) servings.

Calories 182, protein 10.7 gm, sugars 3.1 gm, fiber 16.1 gm, sat. fat .34 gm, poly. fat 1.18 mg, choles. 0 mg, sodium 293.8 mg, potas. 608.3 mg. Analysis for ¹/₉ of recipe.

SOUPS

HAPPY HOME RECIPE

4 c. love
2 c. loyalty
3 c. forgiveness
1 c. friendship
5 T. hope
2 T. tenderness
4 qts. faith
1 barrel laughter

Take love and loyalty, mix it well with faith. Blend with tenderness, kindness and understanding. Add the friendship and hope; sprinkle with laughter. Bake it with sunshine. Serve daily with generous helpings.

BLACK BEAN CHILI

1¹/₂ c. black beans
2 c. onion, chopped & divided
1¹/₂ tsp. garlic powder
2 (16-oz.) cans whole tomatoes, chopped &
  undrained
1 lb. hamburger
1 green pepper, chopped
1 tsp. pepper
2 T. chili powder
1¹/₂ T. cumin
¹/₈ tsp. crushed red pepper

In large kettle, cover black beans with water and bring to a boil. Turn off heat and let stand 1 hour. Add 1¹/₂ cups onion and garlic. Simmer till beans are tender. Drain. Add tomatoes. Brown hamburger with ¹/₂ cup onion, green pepper, pepper, chili powder, cumin and red pepper. Drain fat and add meat mixture to beans. Heat through. Serve with accompaniments such as tortilla chips, 1 cup grated cheese, 1 cup thinly sliced lettuce, 1 mashed avocado and ¹/₂ cup sour cream. **Option:** Omit meat, use ¹/₂ cup onion as topping.

Calories 362, protein 26.75 gm, sugars 4.8 gm, fiber 18.6 gm, sat. fat 4.6 gm, poly. fat .76 mg, choles. 50.6 mg, sodium 48.8 mg, potas. 940 mg. Analysis for ¹/₈ of recipe.

SOUTH OF THE BORDER BLACK BEAN SOUP

1 1/2 c. black beans
6 c. chicken broth
2 T. margarine
1 c. celery, chopped
1 c. onion, chopped
1 c. carrots, grated
1/2 c. potatoes, grated
1 bay leaf
1/2 tsp. garlic powder
1 tsp. oregano
1/2 tsp. pepper
3 T. lemon juice

Wash and soak beans; drain. Put in large pan with chicken broth; heat to boiling. Reduce heat and simmer 3 hours. In large skillet, saute onion, celery and carrots in margarine till tender. Add to beans, with potatoes, bay leaf, garlic powder, oregano and pepper. Stir well and simmer 1 hour more or till vegetables are tender. Stir in lemon juice at serving time.

Calories 321, protein 20.8 gm, sugars 2.6 gm, fiber 24 gm, sat. fat .83 gm, poly. fat 1.46 mg, choles. 2 mg, sodium 842.5 mg, potas. 1015.6 mg. Analysis for 1/6 of recipe.

SOUPS

HOLIDAY BLACK BEAN SOUP

1 1/2 c. black beans
1/2 lb. bacon, cut up
3 c. chicken broth
2 T. salad oil
2 c. carrots, chopped
2 c. onions, chopped
1 c. celery, chopped
1/2 tsp. garlic powder
1/4 tsp. ground cloves
1 (4-oz.) can green chilies
3 T. lime juice
1 lb. chorizo sausage
6 T. cilantro or parsley

Put beans with bacon and broth in a large pan. Add water to cover beans by 1 inch. Cook 1 hour. Saute veggies in oil. Add to beans and cook 1 1/2 hours or till tender. Cook sausage; drain grease. Drain beans, reserving liquid. Puree beans; add some of the reserved liquid to make a thick soup. Reheat soup and add lime juice. Put sausage in bowls; add soup and sprinkle with cilantro. **Option:** Add 1 cup dry sherry with the lime juice.

Calories 513, protein 26.25 gm, sugars 2.13 gm, fiber 18.6 gm, sat. fat 9.26 gm, poly. fat 4.7 mg, choles. 48 mg, sodium 1082.5 mg, potas. 982 mg. Analysis for 1/8 of recipe.

SOUPS

Recipe Favorites

INDEX OF RECIPES

SOUPS

ORDER FORM FOR MITIE MIXES

Please send a check or money order to Mitie Mixes, Inc.
2100 W. Drake #295, Ft. Collins, CO 80526.
CALICO SOUP MIX _____ pkgs. $1.50 each _____
FIESTA SOUP MIX _____ pkgs. $1.50 each _____
BLACK BEANS _____ pkgs. $1.50 each _____
Shipping & handling:
1 to 3 mixes, add $1.00 for each unit.
4 to 6 mixes, add $ .90 for each unit.
7 or more mixes, add $ .35 for each unit.
                          Total enclosed _____
Allow 4 to 6 weeks for delivery.
Price includes any applicable sales tax.

Please type or print

Name_____

Address_____

City_____

State _____ Zip _____

ORDER FORM FOR MITIE MIXES

Please send a check or money order to Mitie Mixes, Inc.
2100 W. Drake #295, Ft. Collins, CO 80526.
CALICO SOUP MIX _____ pkgs. $1.50 each _____
FIESTA SOUP MIX _____ pkgs. $1.50 each _____
BLACK BEANS _____ pkgs. $1.50 each _____
Shipping & handling
1 to 3 mixes, add $1.00 for each unit.
4 to 6 mixes, add $ .90 for each unit.
7 or more mixes, add $ .35 for each unit.
                          Total enclosed _____
Allow 4 to 6 weeks for delivery.
Price includes any applicable sales tax.

Please type or print

Name_____

Address_____

City_____

State _____ Zip _____

Order a book for a friend...
It's a Perfect Gift!

ORDER FORM

For additional copies of this cookbook contact:

**More Than Soup Bean Cookbook
2100 W. Drake #295
Ft. Collins, CO 80526**

Please mail me _____ copies of your More Than Soup Bean Cookbook $7.95 per copy plus $1.50 for shipping and handling per book. Enclosed is my check or money order for $_____.

Mail books to:

Name_____

Address_____

City_____State_____Zip_____

- -

Please mail me _____ copies of your More Than Soup Bean Cookbook $7.95 per copy plus $1.50 for shipping and handling per book. Enclosed is my check or money order for $_____.

Mail books to:

Name_____

Address_____

City_____State_____Zip_____

COOKING TIPS

- After stewing a chicken for diced meat for casseroles, etc., let cool in broth before cutting into chunks–it will have twice the flavor.

- To slice meat into thin strips, as for Chinese dishes–partially freeze and it will slice easily.

- A roast with the bone in will cook faster than a boneless roast–the bone carries the heat to the inside of the roast quicker.

- Never cook a roast cold–let stand for a least an hour at room temperature. Brush with oil before and during roasting–the oil will seal in the juices.

- For a juicier hamburger add cold water to the beef before grilling (1/2 cup to 1 pound of meat).

- To freeze meatballs, place them on a cookie sheet until frozen. Place in plastic bags and they will stay separated so that you may remove as many as you want.

- To keep cauliflower white while cooking–add a little milk to the water.

- When boiling corn, add sugar to the water instead of salt. Salt will toughen the corn.

- To ripen tomatoes–put them in a brown paper bag in a dark pantry and they will ripen overnight.

- Do not use soda to keep vegetables green. It destroys Vitamin C.

- When cooking cabbage, place a small tin cup or can half full of vinegar on the stove near the cabbage. It will absorb all odor from it.

- Potatoes soaked in salt water for 20 minutes before baking will bake more rapidly.

- Let raw potatoes stand in cold water for at least half an hour before frying to improve the crispness of French fried potatoes.

- Use greased muffin tins as molds when baking stuffed green peppers.

- A few drops of lemon juice in the water will whiten boiled potatoes.

- Buy mushrooms before they "open." When stems and caps are attached snugly, mushrooms are truly fresh.

- Do not use metal bowls when mixing salads. Use wooden, glass or china.

- Lettuce keeps better if you store in refrigerator without washing first so that the leaves are dry. Wash the day you are going to use.

- To keep celery crisp–stand it up in a pitcher of cold, salted water and refrigerate.

- Don't despair if you've oversalted the gravy. Stir in some instant mashed potatoes and you'll repair the damage. Just add a little more liquid to offset the thickening.

CALORIE  COUNTER

Beverages

Apple juice, 6 oz. 90
Coffee (black/unsw.) 0
Cola type, 12 oz. 115
Cranberry juice, 6 oz. 115
Ginger ale, 12 oz. 115
Grape juice, (prepared from
   frozen concentrate), 6 oz. 142
Lemonade (prepared from
   frozen concentrate), 6 oz. 85
Milk
   protein fortified, 1 c. 105
   skim, 1 c. 90
   whole, 1 c. 160
Orange juice, 6 oz. 85
Pineapple juice, unsweetened, 6 oz....95
Root beer, 12 oz. 150
Tonic (quinine water), 12 oz. 132

Breads

Corn Bread, 1 small square 130
Dumplings, 1 med. 70
French Toast, 1 slice 135
Muffins
   bran, 1 muffin 106
   blueberry, 1 muffin 110
   corn, 1 muffin 125
   English, 1 muffin 280
Melba Toast, 1 slice 25
Pancakes, 1-4 in. 60
Pumpernickel, 1 slice 75
Rye, 1 slice 60
Waffles, 1 216
White, 1 slice 60-70
Whole wheat, 1 slice 55-65

Cereals

Corn Flakes, 1 cup. 105
Cream of Wheat, 1 cup 120
Oatmeal, 1 cup 148
Rice Flakes, 1 cup 105
Shredded Wheat, 1 biscuit 100
Sugar Krisps, 3/4 cup 110

Crackers

Graham, 1 cracker 15-30
Rye Crisp, 1 cracker 35
Saltine, 1 cracker 17-20
Wheat Thins, 1 cracker 9

Dairy Products

Butter or Margarine, 1 T 100
Cheese
   American Cheese, 1 oz. 100
   Camembert, 1 oz. 85
   Cheddar, 1 oz. 115
   Cottage Cheese, 1 oz. 30
   Mozzarella, 1 oz. 90
   Parmesan, 1 oz. 130
   Ricotta, 1 oz. 50
   Roquefort, 1 oz. 105
   Swiss, 1 oz. 105
Cream
   Light, 1 T 30
   Heavy, 1 T. 55
   Sour, 1 T 45
Hot chocolate, with milk, 1 c. 277
Milk chocolate, 1 oz. 145-155
Yogurt
   made w/ whole milk, 1 c. 150-165
   made w/ skimmed milk, 1 c. 125

Eggs

Fried, 1 large 100
Poached or boiled, 1 large 75-80
Scrambled or in omelet, 1 large..110-130

Fish and Seafood

Bass, 4 oz. 105
Salmon, broiled or baked, 3 oz. 155
Sardines canned in oil, 3 oz. 170
Trout, fried, 3 1/2 oz. 220
Tuna, in oil, 3 oz. 170
Tuna, in water, 3 oz. 110

Calorie Counter, Continued

Fruits

Apple, 1 medium 80-100
Applesauce, sweetened, 1/2 c. 90-115
Applesauce, unsweetened,
    1/2 c. 50
Banana, 1 medium 85
Blueberries, 1/2 c. 45
Cantaloupe melon, 1/2 c. 24
Cherries (pitted), raw, 1/2 c. 40
Grapefruit, 1/2 medium 55
Grapes, 1/2 c. ....35 - 55
Honeydew melon, 1/2 c. 55
Mango, 1 medium 90
Orange, 1 medium 65-75
Peach, 1 medium 35
Pear, 1 medium 60-100
Pineapple, fresh, 1/2 c. 40
Pineapple, canned in syrup, 1/2 c. 95
Plum, 1 medium 30
Strawberries, fresh, 1/2 c. 30
Strawberries, frozen
    and sweetened, 1/2 c. 120-140
Tangerine, 1 large 39
Watermelon, 1/2 c. 42

Meat and Poultry

Beef, ground (lean), 3 oz. 185
Beef, roast, 3 oz. 185
Chicken, broiled, 3 oz. 115
Lamb chop (lean), 3 oz. 175-200
Sirloin steak, 3 oz. 175
Tenderloin steak, 3 oz. 174
Top round steak, 3 oz. 162
Turkey, dark meat, 3 oz. 175
Turkey, white meat, 3 oz. 150
Veal cutlet, 3 oz. 156
Veal, roast, 3 oz. 176

Nuts

Almonds, 2 T. 105
Cashews, 2 T. 100
Peanuts, 2 T. 105
Peanut butter, 1 T. 95
Pecans, 2 T. 95
Pistachios, 2 T. 92
Walnuts, 2 T. 80

Pasta

Macaroni or spaghetti,
    3/4 c. cooked 115

Salad Dressings

Blue cheese, 1 T. 70
French, 1 T. 65
Italian, 1 T. 80
Mayonnaise, 1 T. 100
Olive oil, 1 T. 124
Russian, 1 T. 70
Salad oil, 1 T. 120

Soups

Bean, 1 c. 130-180
Beef noodle, 1 c. 70
Bouillon and consomme, 1 c. 30
Chicken noodle, 1 c. 65
Chicken with rice, 1 c. 50
Minestrone, 1 c. 80-150
Split pea, 1 c. 145-170
Tomato with milk, 1 c. 170
Vegetable, 1 c. 80-100

Vegetables

Asparagus, 1 c. 35
Broccoli, cooked, 1/2 c. 25
Cabbage, cooked, 1/2 c. 15-20
Carrots, cooked, 1/2 c. 25-30
Cauliflower, 1/2 c. 10-15
Corn (kernels), 1/2 c. 70
Green Beans, 1 c. 30
Lettuce, shredded, 1/2 c. 5
Mushrooms, canned, 1/2 c. 20
Onions, cooked, 1/2 c. 30
Peas, green, cooked, 1/2 c. 60
Potato
    baked, 1 medium 90
    chips, 8-10 100
    mashed, with milk
    and butter, 1 c. 200-300
Spinach, 1 cup 40
Tomato
    raw, 1 medium 25
    cooked, 1/2 c. 30

MEASUREMENTS & SUBSTITUTIONS

Measurements

a pinch	1/8 teaspoon or less
3 teaspoons	1 tablespoon
4 tablespoons	1/4 cup
8 tablespoons	1/2 cup
12 tablespoons	3/4 cup
16 tablespoons	1 cup
2 cups	1 pint
4 cups	1 quart
4 quarts	1 gallon
8 quarts	1 peck
4 pecks	1 bushel
16 ounces	1 pound
32 ounces	1 quart
8 ounces liquid	1 cup
1 ounce liquid	2 tablespoons

(For liquid and dry measurements use standard measuring spoons and cups. All measurements are level.)

Substitutions

Ingredient	Quantity	Substitute
self rising flour	1 cup	1 cup all-purpose flour, 1/2 tsp. salt, and 1 tsp. baking powder
cornstarch	1 tablespoon	2 T. flour or 2 tsp. quick-cooking tapioca
baking powder	1 teaspoon	1/4 tsp. baking soda plus 1/2 tsp. cream of tartar
powdered sugar	1 cup	1 c. granulated sugar plus 1 tsp. cornstarch
brown sugar	1/2 cup	2 T. molasses in 1/2 c. granulated sugar
sour milk	1 cup	1 T. lemon juice or vinegar plus sweet milk to make 1 c. (let stand 5 minutes).
whole milk	1 cup	1/2 c. evaporated milk plus 1/2 c. water
cracker crumbs	3/4 cup	1 c. bread crumbs
chocolate	1 square (1 oz.)	3 or 4 T. cocoa plus 1 T. butter*
fresh herbs	1 tablespoon	1 tsp. dried herbs
fresh onion	1 small	1 T. instant minced onion, rehydrated
dry mustard	1 teaspoon	1 T. prepared mustard
tomato juice	1 cup	1/2 c. tomato sauce plus 1/2 c. water
catsup or chili sauce	1 cup	1 c. tomato sauce plus 1/2 c. sugar and 2 T. vinegar (for use in cooking).
dates	1 lb.	1 1/2 c. dates, pitted and cut
bananas	3 medium	1 c. mashed
min. marshmallows	10	1 lg. marshmallow

*In substituting cocoa for chocolate in cakes, the amount of flour must be reduced.
Brown and White Sugars: Usually may be used interchangeably.

MICROWAVE HINTS

1. Place an open box of hardened brown sugar in the microwave oven with 1 cup hot water. Microwave at high for 1 1/2 to 2 minutes for 1/2 pound or 2 to 3 minutes for 1 pound.
2. Soften hard ice cream by microwaving at 30% power. One pint will take 15 to 30 seconds; one quart, 30-45 seconds; and one-half gallon 45-60 seconds.
3. One stick of butter or margarine will soften in 1 minute when microwaved at 20% power.
4. Soften one 8-ounce package of cream cheese by microwaving at 30% power for 2 to 2 1/2 minutes. One 3-ounce package of cream cheese will soften in 1 1/2 to 2 minutes.
5. Thaw frozen orange juice right in the container. Remove the top metal lid. Place the opened container in the microwave and heat on high power 30 seconds for 6 ounces and 45 seconds for 12 ounces.
6. Thaw whipped topping…a 4 1/2 ounce carton will thaw in 1 minute on the defrost setting. Whipped topping should be slightly firm in the center but it will blend well when stirred. Do not overthaw!
7. Soften Jello that has set up too hard–perhaps you were to chill it until slightly thickened and forgot it. Heat on a low power setting for a very short time.
8. Heat hot packs in a microwave oven. A wet finger tip towel will take about 25 seconds. It depends on the temperature of the water used to wet the towel.
9. To scald milk, cook 1 cup for 2 to 2 1/2 minutes, stirring once each minute.
10. To make dry bread crumbs, cut 6 slices bread into 1/2-inch cubes. Microwave in 3-quart casserole 6-7 minutes, or until dry, stirring after 3 minutes. Crush in blender.
11. Refresh stale potato chips, crackers or other snacks of such type by putting a plateful in the microwave oven for about 30-45 seconds. Let stand for 1 minute to crisp. Cereals can also be crisped.
12. Nuts will be easier to shell if you place 2 cups of nuts in a 1-quart casserole with 1 cup of water. Cook for 4 to 5 minutes and the nutmeats will slip out whole after cracking the shell.
13. For stamp collectors: place a few drops of water on stamp to be removed from envelope. Heat in the microwave for 20 seconds and the stamp will come right off.
14. Using a round dish instead of a square one eliminates overcooked corners in baking cakes.
15. A crusty coating of chopped walnuts surrounding many microwave cooked cakes and quick breads enhances the looks and eating quality. Sprinkle a layer of medium, finely chopped walnuts evenly onto the bottom and side of a ring pan or bundt cake pan. Pour in batter and microwave as recipe directs.
16. Do not salt foods on the surface as it causes dehydration and toughens the food. Salt after you remove from the oven unless the recipe calls for using salt in the mixture.
17. Heat left-over custard and use it as frosting for a cake.
18. Melt marshmallow cream in the microwave oven. Half of a 7-ounce jar will melt in 35-40 seconds on high. Stir to blend.
19. Toast coconut in the microwave. Watch closely as it browns quickly once it begins to brown. Spread 1/2 cup coconut in a pie plate and cook for 3-4 minutes, stirring every 30 seconds after 2 minutes.

Herbs & Spices

Get acquainted with herbs and spices. Add in small amounts, 1/4 teaspoon for each 4 servings. Taste before adding more. Crush dried herbs or snip fresh herbs before using. If substituting fresh for dried, use 3 times more fresh herbs.

Basil Sweet warm flavor with an aromatic odor, used whole or ground. Good with lamb, fish, roast, stews, ground beef, vegetables, dressing and omelets.

Bay Leaves A pungent flavor, use whole leaf but remove before serving. Good in vegetable dishes, fish and seafood, stews and pickles.

Caraway Has a spicy smell and aromatic taste. Use in cakes, breads, soups, cheese and sauerkraut.

Chives Sweet mild flavor of onion, this herb is excellent in salads, fish, soups and potatoes.

Curry Powder A number of spices combined to proper proportions to give a distinct flavor to such dishes as meat, poultry, fish and vegetables.

Dill Both seeds and leaves of dill are flavorful. Leaves may be used to garnish or cook with fish, soup, dressings, potatoes and beans. Leaves or the whole plant may be used to spice dill pickles.

Fennel Both seeds and leaves are used. It has a sweet hot flavor. Use in small quantities in pies and baked goods. Leaves can be boiled with fish.

Ginger A pungent root, this aromatic spice is sold fresh, dried, or ground. Used in pickles, preserves, cakes, cookies, soups and meat dishes.

Herbs & Spices

Marjoram   May be used both dry or green. Used to flavor fish, poultry, omelets, lamb, stew, stuffing and tomato juice.

Mint   Leaves are aromatic with a cool flavor. Excellent in beverages, fish, cheese, lamb, soup, peas, carrots, and fruit desserts.

Oregano   Strong aromatic odor, use whole or ground to spice tomato juice, fish, eggs, pizza, omelets, chili, stew, gravy, poultry and vegetables.

Paprika   A bright red pepper, this spice is used in meat, vegetables and soups. Can be used as a garnish for potatoes, salads or eggs.

Parsley   Best when used fresh but can be used dry. Use as garnish or seasoning. Try in fish, omelets, soup, meat, stuffing and mixed greens.

Rosemary   Very aromatic, used fresh or dried. Season fish, stuffing, beef, lamb, poultry, onions, eggs and bread.

Saffron   Orange yellow in color, this spice is used to flavor or color foods. Use in soup, chicken, rice and fancy breads.

Sage   Use fresh or dried. The flowers are sometimes used in salads. May be used in tomato juice, fish, fondue, omelets, beef, poultry, stuffing, cheese spreads, cornbread and biscuits.

Tarragon   Leaves have a pungent, hot taste. Use to flavor sauces, salads, meat, poultry, tomatoes and dressings.

NAPKIN FOLDING

General Tips:
Use linen napkins if possible, well starched.
For the more complicated folds, 24 inch napkins work best.
Practice the folds with newspapers.
Children can help. Once they learn the folds, they will have fun!

Shield
This fold is easy. Elegant with Monogram in Corner.

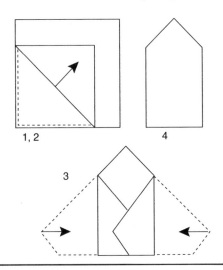

Instructions:
1. Fold into quarter size. If monogrammed, ornate corner should face down.
2. Turn up folded corner three-quarters.
3. Overlap right and left side points.
4. Turn over; adjust sides so that they are even, single point in center.
5. Place point up or down on plate, or left of plate.

Rosette
Elegant on Plate.

Instructions:
1. Fold top and bottom edges to the center, leaving 1/2" opening along the center.
2. Pleat firmly from the left edge. Sharpen edges with hot iron.
3. Pinch center together. If necessary, use small piece of pipe cleaner to secure and top with single flower.
4. Spread out rosette.

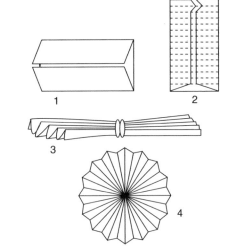

NAPKIN FOLDING

Fan

Pretty in Napkin Ring, or Top of Plate.

Instructions:
1. Fold top and bottom edges to the center.
2. Fold top and bottom edges to center a second time.
3. Pleat firmly from the left edge. Sharpen edges with a hot iron.
4. Spread out fan. Balance flat folds on each side on table. Well-starched napkins will hold the shape.

Candle

Easy to do; can be decorated.

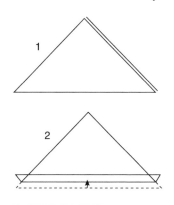

Instructions:
1. Fold into triangle, point at top.
2. Turn lower edge up 1".
3. Turn over, folded edge down.
4. Roll tightly from left to right.
5. Tuck in corner. Stand upright.

Lily

Effective and Pretty on Table.

Instructions:
1. Fold napkin into quarters.
2. Fold into triangle, closed corner to open points.
3. Turn two points over to other side. (Two points are on either side of closed point.) Pleat.
4. Place closed end in glass. Pull down two points on each side and shape.

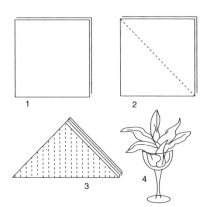

VEGETABLE TIME TABLE

Vegetable	Cooking Method	Time
Asparagus Tips	Boiled..................	10-15 minutes
Artichokes, French	Boiled..................	40 minutes
	Steamed...............	45-60 minutes
Beans, Lima	Boiled..................	20-40 minutes
	Steamed...............	60 minutes
Beans, String	Boiled..................	15-35 minutes
	Steamed...............	60 minutes
Beets, young with skin	Boiled..................	30 minutes
	Steamed...............	60 minutes
	Baked..................	70-90 minutes
Beets, old	Boiled or Steamed...	1-2 hours
Broccoli, flowerets	Boiled..................	5-10 minutes
Broccoli, stems	Boiled..................	20-30 minutes
Brussel Sprouts	Boiled..................	20-30 minutes
Cabbage, chopped	Boiled..................	10-20 minutes
	Steamed...............	25 minutes
Cauliflower, stem down	Boiled..................	20-30 minutes
Cauliflower, flowerets	Boiled..................	8-10 minutes
Carrots, cut across	Boiled..................	8-10 minutes
	Steamed...............	40 minutes
Corn, green, tender	Boiled..................	5-10 minutes
	Steamed...............	15 minutes
	Baked..................	20 minutes
Corn on the cob	Boiled..................	8-10 minutes
	Steamed...............	15 minutes
Eggplant, whole	Boiled..................	30 minutes
	Steamed...............	40 minutes
	Baked..................	45 minutes
Parsnips	Boiled..................	25-40 minutes
	Steamed...............	60 minutes
	Baked..................	60-75 minutes
Peas, green	Boiled or Steamed...	5-15 minutes
Potatoes	Boiled..................	20-40 minutes
	Steamed...............	60 minutes
	Baked..................	45-60 minutes
Pumpkin or Squash	Boiled..................	20-40 minutes
	Steamed...............	45 minutes
	Baked..................	60 minutes
Tomatoes	Boiled..................	5-15 minutes
Turnips	Boiled..................	25-40 minutes

BUYING GUIDE
Fresh Vegetables and Fruits

Experience is the best teacher in choosing quality, but here are a few pointers on buying some of the fruits and vegetables.

Asparagus: Stalks should be tender and firm, tips should be close and compact. Choose the stalks with very little white–they are more tender. Use asparagus soon–it toughens rapidly.

Beans, Snap: Those with small seeds inside the pods are best. Avoid beans with dry-looking pods.

Berries: Select plump, solid berries with good color. Avoid stained containers, indicating wet or leaky berries. Berries such as blackberries and raspberries with clinging caps may be under-ripe. Strawberries without caps may be too ripe.

Broccoli, Brussel Sprouts, and Cauliflower: Flower clusters on broccoli and cauliflower should be tight and close together. Brussel sprouts should be firm and compact. Smudgy, dirty spots may indicate insects.

Cabbage and Head Lettuce: Choose heads heavy for size. Avoid cabbage with worm holes, lettuce with discoloration or soft rot.

Cucumbers: Choose long, slender cucumbers for best quality. May be dark or medium green but yellowed ones are undesirable.

Melons: In cantaloupes, thick close netting on the rind indicates best quality. Cantaloupes are ripe when the stem scar is smooth and space between the netting is yellow or yellow-green. They are best when fully ripe with fruity odor.

Honeydews are ripe when rind has creamy to yellowish color and velvety texture. Immature honeydews are whitish-green.

Ripe watermelons have some yellow color on one side. If melons are white or pale green on one side, they are not ripe.

Oranges, Grapefruit, and Lemons: Choose those heavy for their size. Smoother, thinner skins usually indicate more juice. Most skin markings do not affect quality. Oranges with a slight greenish tinge may be just as ripe as fully colored ones. Light or greenish-yellow lemons are more tart than deep yellow ones. Avoid citrus fruits showing withered, sunken, or soft areas.

Peas and Lima Beans: Select pods that are well-filled but not bulging. Avoid dried, spotted, yellowed, or flabby pods.

TABLE FOR DRIED FRUITS		
Fruit	**Cooking Time**	**Amount of Sugar or Honey**
Apricots	About 40 minutes	1/4 c. for each cup of fruit
Figs	About 30 minutes	1 T. for each cup of fruit
Peaches	About 45 minutes	1/4 c. for each cup of fruit
Prunes	About 45 minutes	2 T. for each cup of fruit

BAKING PERFECT BREADS

Proportions

Biscuits ....To 1 c. flour use 1 1/4 tsp. Baking Powder
Muffins ....To 1 c. flour use 1 1/2 tsp. Baking Powder
Popovers..To 1 c. flour use 1 1/4 tsp. Baking Powder
Waffles ....To 1 c. flour use 1 1/4 tsp. Baking Powder
Cake with oil...To 1 c. flour use 1 tsp. Baking Powder

Rules for Use of Leavening Agents

1. To 1 teaspoon soda use 2 1/4 teaspoons cream of tartar, or 2 cups freshly soured milk, or 1 cup molasses.

2. In simple flour mixtures, use 2 teaspoons baking powder to leaven 1 cup flour. Reduce this amount 1/2 teaspoon for each egg used.

3. To substitute soda and an acid for baking powder, divide the amount of baking powder by 4. Take that as your measure of and add the acid according to rule 1 above.

Proportions for Batters and Dough

Pour Batter ....To 1 cup liquid use 1 cup flour
Drop Batter..............................To 1 cup liquid use 2 to 2 1/2 cups flour
Soft Dough ....To 1 cup liquid use 3 to 3 1/2 cups flour
Stiff Dough ....To 1 cup liquid use 4 cups flour

Hints for Baking Breads

Kneading the dough for a half minute after mixing improves the texture of baking powder biscuits.

Use cooking or salad oil in waffles and hot cakes in the place of shortening. No extra pan or bowl to melt the shortening and no waiting.

When bread is baking, a small dish of water in the oven will help to keep the crust from getting hard.

Dip the spoon in hot water to measure shortening, butter, etc., the fat will slip out more easily.

Small amounts of leftover corn may be added to pancake batter for variety.

To make bread crumbs, use fine cutter of the food grinder and tie a large paper bag over the spout to prevent flying crumbs.

When you are doing any sort of baking, you get better results if you remember to pre-heat your cookie sheet, muffin tins, or cake pans.

Oven Temperature Chart

Breads	Minutes	Temperature
Loaf	45 - 60	350° - 400°
Rolls	15 - 30	350° - 425°
Biscuits	10 - 15	400° - 450°
Muffins	15 - 25	400° - 425°
Cornbread	20 - 25	400° - 425°
Nut Bread	60 - 75	350°
Gingerbread	35 - 50	350° - 375°

BAKING PERFECT DESSERTS

For Perfect Cookies

Cookie dough that is to be rolled is much easier to handle after it has been refrigerated for 10 to 30 minutes. This keeps the dough from sticking, even though it may be soft. If not done, the soft dough may require more flour and too much flour makes cookies hard and brittle. In rolling, take out on a floured board, only as much dough as can be easily managed. Flour the rolling pin slightly and roll lightly to desired thickness. Cut shapes close together and keep all trimmings for the last roll. Place pans or sheets in upper third of oven. Watch cookies carefully while baking to avoid burning edges. When sprinkling sugar on cookies, try putting it into a salt shaker. It saves time.

For Perfect Pies and Cakes

- A pie crust will be more easily made and better if all the ingredients are cool.

- The lower crust should be placed in the pan so that it covers the surface smoothly. Be sure no air lurks beneath the surface, for it will push the crust out of shape in baking.

- Folding the top crust over the lower crust before crimping will keep the juices in the pie.

- In making custard type pies, bake at a high temperature for about ten minutes to prevent a soggy crust. Then finish baking at a low temperature.

- Fill cake pans about 2/3 full and spread batter well into corners and to the sides, leaving a slight hollow in the center.

- The cake is done when it shrinks from the sides of the pan or if it springs back when touched lightly with the finger.

- After a cake comes from the oven, it should be placed on a rack for about five minutes. Then the sides should be loosened and the cake turned out on a rack to finish cooling.

- Cakes should not be frosted until thoroughly cool.

- To prevent crust from becoming soggy with cream pie, sprinkle crust with powdered sugar.

Temperature Chart

Food	Temperature	Time
Butter Cake, loaf	300° - 350°	50 - 80 min.
Butter Cake, layer	350° - 375°	25 - 35 min.
Cake, angel	350° - 375°	35 - 50 min.
Cake, sponge	350° - 375°	12 - 40 min.
Cake, fruit	250° - 275°	3 - 4 hours
Cookies, rolled	375° - 400°	6 - 12 min.
Cookies, drop	350° - 400°	8 - 15 min.
Cream Puffs	300° - 350°	45 - 60 min.
Meringue	300° - 350°	12 - 15 min.
Pie Crust (shell)	400° - 450°	10 - 12 min.

Food Quantities for Serving 25, 50, and 100 People

Food	25 Servings	50 Servings	100 Servings
Sandwiches:			
Bread	50 slices or 3 (1-lb.) loaves	100 slices or 6 (1-lb.) loaves	200 slices or 12 (1-lb.) loaves
Butter	1/2 pound	3/4 to 1 pound	1 1/2 pounds
Mayonnaise	1 cup	2 to 3 cups	4 to 6 cups
Mixed Filling (meat, eggs, fish)	1 1/2 quarts	2 1/2 to 3 quarts	5 to 6 quarts
Mixed Filling (sweet-fruit)	1 quart	1 3/4 to 2 quarts	2 1/2 to 4 quarts
Lettuce	1 1/2 heads	2 1/2 to 3 heads	5 to 6 heads
Meat, Poultry, or Fish:			
Hot dogs (beef)	6 1/2 pounds	13 pounds	25 pounds
Hamburger	9 pounds	18 pounds	35 pounds
Turkey or Chicken	13 pounds	25 to 35 pounds	50 to 75 pounds
Fish, large whole (round)	13 pounds	25 pounds	50 pounds
Fish fillets or steak	7 1/2 pounds	15 pounds	30 pounds
Salads, Casseroles:			
Potato Salad	4 1/4 quarts	1 1/4 gallons	4 1/4 gallons
Scalloped Potatoes	4 1/2 quarts or 1 12" x 20" pan	8 1/2 quarts	17 quarts
Spaghetti	1 1/4 gallons	2 1/2 gallons	5 gallons
Baked Beans	3/4 gallon	1 1/4 gallons	2 1/2 gallons
Jello Salad	3/4 gallon	1 1/4 gallons	2 1/2 gallons
Ice Cream:			
Brick	3 1/4 quarts	6 1/2 quarts	12 1/2 quarts
Bulk	2 1/4 quarts	4 1/2 quarts or 1 1/4 gallons	9 quarts or 2 1/2 gallons
Beverages:			
Coffee	1/2 pound and 1 1/2 gal. water	1 pound and 3 gal. water	2 pounds and 6 gal. water
Tea	1/12 pound and 1 1/2 gal. water	1/6 pound 3 gal. water	1/3 pound and 6 gal. water
Lemonade	10 to 15 lemons, 1 1/2 gal. water	20 to 30 lemons, 3 gal. water	40 to 60 lemons, 6 gal. water
Desserts:			
Watermelon	37 1/2 pounds	75 pounds	150 pounds
Cake	1 10" x 12" sheet cake 2 8" layer cakes	1 12" x 20" sheet cakes 3 10" layer cakes	2 12" x 20" sheet cakes 6 10" layer cakes
Whipping Cream	1 pint	1 quart	2 quarts

EQUIVALENCY CHART

FOOD	QUANTITY	YIELD
unsifted flour	3 3/4 cups	1 pound
sifted flour	4 cups	1 pound
sifted cake flour	4 1/2 cups	1 pound
rye flour	5 cups	1 pound
flour	1 pound	4 cups
baking powder	5 1/2 ounces	1 cup
cornmeal	3 cups	1 pound
cornstarch	3 cups	1 pound
lemon	1 medium	3 tablespoons juice
apple	1 medium	1 cup
orange	3-4 medium	1 cup juice
onion	1 medium	1/2 cup
unshelled walnuts	1 pound	1 1/2 to 1 3/4 cups
sugar	2 cups	1 pound
powdered sugar	3 1/2 cups	1 pound
brown sugar	2 1/2 cups	1 pound
spaghetti	7 ounces	4 cups cooked
noodles (uncooked)	4 ounces (1 1/2 - 2 cups)	2-3 cups cooked
macaroni (uncooked)	4 ounces (1 1/4 cups)	2 1/4 cups cooked
macaroni (cooked)	6 cups	8-ounce package
noodles (cooked)	7 cups	8-ounce package
long-grain rice (uncooked)	1 cup	3-4 cups cooked
saltine crackers	28 crackers	1 cup fine crumbs
butter	1 stick or 1/4 lb.	1/2 cup
cocoa	4 cups	1 pound
chocolate (bitter)	1 ounce	1 square
coconut	2 2/3 cups	1 1/2 pound carton
marshmallows	16	1/4 pound
graham crackers	14 squares	1 cup fine crumbs
vanilla wafers	22	1 cup fine crumbs
bread	1 1/2 slices	1 cup soft crumbs
bread	1 slice	1/4 cup fine, dry crumbs
egg whites	8-10	1 cup
egg yolks	10-12	1 cup
egg	4-5 whole	1 cup
flavored gelatin	3 1/4 ounces	1/2 cup
unflavored gelatin	1/4 ounce	1 tablespoon
nuts (chopped)	1 cup	1/4 pound
almonds	3 1/2 cups	1 pound
walnuts (broken)	3 cups	1 pound
raisins	1 pound	3 1/2 cups
rice	2 1/3 cups	1 pound
American cheese (grated)	5 cups	1 pound
American cheese (cubed)	2 2/3 cups	1 pound
cream cheese	6 2/3 tablespoons	3-ounce package
zwieback (crumbled)	4	1 cup
banana (mashed)	1 medium	1/3 cup
coffee (ground)	5 cups	1 pound
evaporated milk	1 cup	3 cups whipped

TERMS USED IN COOKING

Au gratin: Topped with crumbs and/or cheese and browned in the oven or under the broiler.

Au jus: Served in its own juices.

Baste: To moisten foods during cooking with pan drippings or special sauce to add flavor and prevent drying.

Bisque: A thick cream soup.

Blanch: To immerse in rapidly boiling water and allow to cook slightly.

Cream: To soften a fat, especially butter, by beating it at room temperature. Butter and sugar are often creamed together, making a smooth, soft paste.

Crimp: To seal the edges of a two-crust pie either by pinching them at intervals with the fingers or by pressing them together with the tines of a fork.

Crudites: An assortment of raw vegetables, i.e. carrots, broccoli, mushrooms, served as an hors d'oeuvre often accompanied by a dip.

Degrease: To remove fat from the surface of stews, soups, or stock. Usually cooled in the refrigerator, so that fat hardens and is easily removed.

Dredge: To coat lightly with flour, cornmeal, etc.

Entree: The main course.

Fold: To incorporate a delicate substance, such as whipped cream or beaten egg whites, into another substance without releasing air bubbles. A spatula is used to gently bring part of the mixture from the bottom of the bowl to the top. The process is repeated, while slowly rotating the bowl, until the ingredients are thoroughly blended.

Glaze: To cover with a glossy coating, such as a melted and somewhat diluted jelly for fruit desserts.

Julienne: To cut vegetables, fruits, or cheeses into match-shaped slivers.

Marinade: To allow food to stand in a liquid to tenderize or to add flavor.

Meuniere: Dredged with flour and sauteed in butter.

Mince: To chop or cut food into very small pieces.

Parboil: To boil until partially cooked; to blanch. Usually this procedure is followed by final cooking in a seasoned sauce.

Pare: To remove the outermost skin of a fruit or vegetable.

Poach: To cook very gently in hot liquid kept just below the boiling point.

Puree: To mash foods until perfectly smooth by hand, by rubbing through a sieve or food mill, or by whirling in a blender or food processor.

Refresh: To run cold water over food that has been parboiled, to stop the cooking process quickly.

Saute: To cook and/or brown food in a small quantity of hot oil.

Scald: To heat to just below the boiling point, when tiny bubbles appear at the edge of the saucepan.

Simmer: To cook in liquid just below the boiling point. The surface of the liquid should be barely moving, broken from time to time by slowly rising bubbles.

Steep: To let food stand in (hot) liquid to extract or to enhance flavor, like tea in hot water or poached fruits in sugar syrup.

Toss: To combine ingredients with a lifting motion.

Whip: To beat rapidly to incorporate air and produce expansion, as in heavy cream or egg whites.